S0-BYI-326

Preaching the
CHRISTIAN YEAR

Preaching the

CHRISTIAN YEAR

HUGHELL E. W. FOSBROKE

ALBERT T. MOLLEGEN

THEODORE O. WEDEL

WILLIAM H. NES

FREDERICK C. GRANT

J. V. LANGMEAD CASSERLEY

W. NORMAN PITTENGER

THEODORE P. FERRIS

Edited for The Dean and Chapter
of the Cathedral Church of St. John the Divine
by

HOWARD A. JOHNSON
CANON THEOLOGIAN

with a Foreword by JAMES A. PIKE
DEAN

CHARLES SCRIBNER'S SONS   *NEW YORK*

© COPYRIGHT 1957 BY THE DEAN AND CHAPTER
OF THE CATHEDRAL CHURCH OF ST. JOHN THE DIVINE

*All rights reserved. No part of this book
may be reproduced in any form without
the permission of Charles Scribner's Sons.*

A–9.57[V]

PRINTED IN THE UNITED STATES OF AMERICA

Library of Congress Catalog Card Number 57-12061

Lit
4600
J6B

133547

BV
4211.2
.J57
1957

FOREWORD

THE TRADITIONAL Christian Year is the Church's safeguard against the idiosyncrasies of its ministers. By spreading the "mighty acts of God" over a span of time each year, it encourages—though it does not guarantee—a balanced diet for the spiritual nurture of the laymen, and it challenges the preacher to encompass all of the essential elements of the Christian message.

But the Christian Year does not limit the freedom of the preacher. Nor does it put words in his mouth. Hence, to encourage preaching according to the Christian Year, the most valuable tool would not seem to be a series of ready-made sermons for the various seasons, but rather a theological analysis of the great themes to which he might address himself during each of the liturgical seasons.

It is this conviction which motivated the Dean and Chapter of the Cathedral Church of St. John the Divine to sponsor last year for the Episcopal Clergy of the greater New York area (but with assurance that they would be of interest to many in all the other communions) a series of lectures by outstanding theologians and preachers, presenting the substance of the *kerygma* and the *didache*, as outlined by the Church calendar. The response to these lectures was such that we concluded that the guidance of these speakers should reach a much larger audience. Hence this book.

We are especially grateful to the authors of these essays, both for their oral and written presentation. We also wish to note with appreciation that the basic idea was suggested by the Reverend Hugh D. McCandless, Rector of the Church of the Epiphany, New York City. The series was organized and the manuscripts were edited by the Canon Theologian of the Cathedral, the Reverend Howard A. Johnson, D.D. In this task he had valuable assistance from the Reverend Richard Reid, Assistant Minister of the Cathedral, and from Miss Caroline Joy, Cathedral Librarian.

My brethren and I hope that the words which follow will provide personal inspiration to the reader—whether minister or layman—and will encourage among the clergy a greater fidelity to the Christian message and the Church Year.

James A. Pike
DEAN OF THE CATHEDRAL CHURCH
OF ST. JOHN THE DIVINE

NEW YORK CITY
FEAST OF THE EPIPHANY, 1957

AN OFFICE FOR PREACHERS

This Office, compiled by the Canon Sacrist, The Reverend Edward N. West, of the Cathedral Church of St. John the Divine, was said by the Clergy in preparation for the hearing of each of the eight lectures on liturgical preaching which compose this book.

Officiant. IN the Name of the Father, and of the Son, and of the Holy Ghost. *Amen.*

Antiphon. O LORD, thy word

I CALL with my whole heart; * hear me, O Lord; I will keep thy statutes.

*Yea, even unto thee do I call; * help me, and I shall keep thy testimonies.*

Early in the morning do I cry unto thee; * for in thy word is my trust.

*Mine eyes prevent the night watches; * that I might be occupied in thy word.*

Hear my voice, O Lord, according unto thy loving-kindness; * quicken me, according to thy judgments.

*They draw nigh that of malice persecute me, * and are far from thy law.*

Be thou nigh at hand, O Lord; * for all thy commandments are true.

*As concerning thy testimonies, I have known long since, * that thou hast grounded them for ever.*

GLORY be to the Father, and to the Son * and to the Holy Ghost;

*As it was in the beginning, is now, and ever shall be, * world without end. Amen.*

Antiphon. O LORD, thy word * endureth for ever in heaven.

Lord, have mercy upon us.
Christ, have mercy upon us.
Lord, have mercy upon us.

OUR Father,
Who art in heaven,
Hallowed be thy Name.
Thy kingdom come.
Thy will be done,
On earth as it is in heaven.
Give us this day our daily bread.
And forgive us our trespasses,
As we forgive those who trespass against us,
And lead us not into temptation,
But deliver us from evil. Amen.

¶ *Then shall all say together*

O LORD my God,
I am not worthy that thou shouldest come under my
    roof;
Yet thou hast honoured thy servant
With appointing him to stand in thy House,
And to serve at thy holy Altar.
To thee and to thy service I devote myself,
Body, soul, and spirit,
With all their powers and faculties.
Fill my memory with the words of thy Law;
Enlighten my understanding
With the illumination of the Holy Ghost;
And may all the wishes and desires of my will
Centre in what thou hast commanded.
And, to make me instrumental in promoting the salva-
    tion
Of the people committed to my charge,
Grant that I may faithfully administer thy holy Sacra-
    ments,
And by my life and doctrine set forth thy true and
    lively Word.
Be ever with me in the performance
Of all the duties of my ministry:
In prayer, to quicken my devotion;
In praises, to heighten my love and gratitude;
And in preaching, to give a readiness of thought and
    expression
Suitable to the clearness and excellency of thy holy
    Word.
Grant this for the sake of Jesus Christ
Thy Son our Saviour. Amen.

Officiant. The Lord be with you.

Answer. *And with thy spirit.*

Let us pray

> O LORD Jesus Christ, who at thy first coming didst send thy messenger to prepare thy way before thee; Grant that the ministers and stewards of thy mysteries may likewise so prepare and make ready thy way, by turning the hearts of the disobedient to the wisdom of the just, that at thy second coming to judge the world we may be found an acceptable people in thy sight, who livest and reignest with the Father and the Holy Spirit ever, one God, world without end. *Amen.*

> THE grace of our Lord Jesus Christ, and the love of God, and the fellowship of the Holy Ghost, be with us all evermore. *Amen.*

CONTENTS

xii CONTENTS

Preaching the
CHRISTIAN YEAR

CHAPTER ONE

Preaching in Advent

BY HUGHELL E. W. FOSBROKE

"AND HE SHALL come again, with glory, to judge both the quick and the dead; Whose kingdom shall have no end." So the Nicene Creed brings to a climax the recital of the incarnate life of our Lord. Following upon the knell-like summing up of his life on earth, "he suffered, and was buried," there is sounded a note of awed rejoicing in the exaltation of Christ, rehearsed in successive stages, his Resurrection, his Ascension, and then the victorious consummation of his work as he enters upon the lordship of a world redeemed and ordered through and through in accordance with his righteous love, a lordship which shall have no end. The parallel with the great passage in St. Paul's Epistle to the Philippians comes at once to mind: "He humbled himself, and became obedient unto death, even the death of the cross. Wherefore God also hath highly exalted him, and given him a name which is above every name: that at the name of Jesus every knee should bow, of things in heaven, and things in earth, and things under the earth; and that every

3

tongue should confess that Jesus Christ is Lord, to the glory of God the Father."

This proclamation of the final and unending triumph of the Christ is the essential note of the Advent message. So in the Collect for the First Sunday in Advent, significantly to be used throughout the Season, the time of this mortal life is characterized as that in which "Jesus Christ came to visit us in great humility," while this same mortal life reaches its fulfilment when "he shall come again in his glorious majesty." The first Christians were no doubt constant in their use of the prayer that Jesus himself had taught them, with the petition "Thy kingdom come!" But a cry that sprang instinctively to their lips as they prayed together has been preserved in that Aramaic tongue which was the native speech of Jesus and his disciples: *Marana tha*, "Our Lord, come!" The Advent hymns with one accord take up the strain: "O come, O come, Emmanuel." "Saviour, take the power and glory, claim the kingdom for Thine own."

It is important to keep clearly in mind this centering on the coming of the King, rather than the coming of the kingdom, as the heart of the Advent hope, for there has been, and apparently will continue to be, much inconclusive debate as to the exact meaning of the phrase, "the kingdom of God," in New Testament usage. It is argued that first and foremost it refers to an eternal sovereignty of God that is always exercising its control. This is in line with Old Testament usage: "The Lord is King; be the people never so impatient. He sitteth between the cherubim; be the earth never so unquiet." Others would think first of all of the presence of the divine sovereignty wherever life is ordered

in accordance with the righteous will of God: "Not everyone that saith unto me, 'Lord, lord!' shall enter into the
kingdom of heaven, but he that doeth the will of my Father
which is in heaven." Again, the kingdom is thought of as
yet to come by the ingress of transcendent power, bringing
with it the consummation of human history in a new age.
Manifestly, there is significant truth in all three interpretations, but it is not easy to hold to concrete realization of a
kingdom which is both present and future, here and still
to come. It is to be remembered, however, that what can
be said about the kingdom derives altogether from what we
know about the King and that God is Personal Being. He
is the living God and it is characteristic of life that it relates
itself actively to its environment, and of personal life in
particular that in so doing it wells up in ever new revelation
of its being.

A very faint analogy of the way in which God, always
present, may yet be said to come may be drawn from ordinary human experience. I take a walk with a friend whom I
greatly admire and revere, and even though we say hardly
anything to each other I find in just the fact that he is with
me a sense of shared enjoyment. Then some word or ges-
ture of his, it may be of flashing indignation at the sight of
a child ill-treated, discloses an unsuspected depth of feeling
in my friend. Or again it may be that in some simple telling
phrase he speaks of the beauty of the landscape, and the
prospect is revealed as something more than the object of
my dull and common seeing. In a sense my friend is still only
there as he was before, but in another and deeper sense he
is come anew into my life and has drawn me into a richer

knowledge of himself and of life's meaning. In some such way, perhaps, we may dare to think of the coming of the King as the breaking in upon the human scene of the living God in Christ in new disclosure of his majesty and power. To be sure, the thought of the coming of God in Christ may still occasion difficulties if there is failure to take seriously (the constant energizing movement of God's will upon and within this world.)

(There is, indeed, a general, if rather vague, belief that God is everywhere present in his universe. But there is also a prevailing tendency to think of this constant presence as if it were unmoving, passively awaiting the acknowledgment that it is always there. Or if there is thought of a divine activity, it is conceived as the exercise of a given quantity of sustaining power. This, of course, falls far short of the Biblical doctrine of a God engaged in ceaseless activity, his creative energy continuously streaming into life, making all things new.)The very verb *to be* in Hebrew has the primary meaning of "becoming" that is instinct with the sense of movement. The familiar passage, "I am that I am," should therefore be rendered "I will be that I will be."

In the non-human world everything from the circling of the stars to the dread mysterious energy at the heart of the atom, from the blade of grass to the "Tiger, tiger, burning bright," is immediately dependent upon the uninterruptedness of the divine activity. "The lions roaring after their prey do seek their meat from God; he taketh away their breath; they die." "Are not two sparrows sold for a farthing? and one of them shall not fall on the ground without your Father." And in the human story all the age-long striving of the race in its amazing achievement and in its pitiable failure has drawn upon the ever-present forth-putting of the divine energy. The life of each individual in every breath he draws is held in being by the embracing presence and power of God. In the exquisitely simple language of the Psalmist, "I lie down and sleep, and get up again in the morning; for the Lord upholds me." Here is surely no thought of a merely passive support.

He is always here with creative power and yet ever and again he comes. Out of the inexhaustible depth of his personal Being by the new act of self-disclosure the God of righteous love reveals himself afresh; and in the light of a new awareness of his presence, and in the strength of a new communication of the divine energy, life is charged with new meaning. But the particular mighty acts come out of the background of God's constant exercise of his power in the sustaining of his world.

It was thus that the way was made ready for the first coming of the King, and the Advent Season at the beginning of the Church's year is the preparation not only for the commemoration of his birth but for the celebration of the whole of his earthly career. The wonderful revelation of God's own Being—that (in the terms of warm, breathing, human experience in a life that accepted all the splendid, though perilous, responsibilities of human freedom, and out of apparent failure and defeat) won love's ultimate victory—was the completion of that disclosure of himself that God had been making both in the outstanding events and in the normal course of the long discipline of Israel's history. That is to say, the first coming of the

King was in keeping with what God had been doing in the past. In reaction from the older delight in finding in the books of the prophets direct prediction of specific incidents in the Gospel narrative, there has been a sad failure to discern the way in which Israel's history did indeed look forward to the Incarnation. Viewed as the record of the divine activity, the Old Testament presents such an account of God's repeated particular relationship of himself to the course of events as inevitably to call for the consummation of his movement manward in the sending of One, the express image of his person, in whom his very self might be actually participant in human history.

This coming of the King, this active sharing of God in Christ in the time process, did indeed mean the opening of a new epoch in history. In the life and ministry of Jesus the power of the kingdom of God was already at work. On this point, Jesus' challenge to the Pharisees is decisive: "If I with the finger of God cast out devils, no doubt the kingdom of God has come upon you." To the disciples of John the Baptist sent to ask him the anxious question, "Art thou the coming one? or do we look for another?" Jesus replied, "The blind receive their sight, and the lame walk, the lepers are cleansed, and the deaf hear, the dead are raised up, and the poor have the gospel preached to them." Dr. Tillich thus paraphrases this reply: "If I am able to heal the deaf and the blind, if I am able to liberate the mentally sick, then a new reality has come upon you." The consummation of the kingdom, the final vindication of the righteousness of God embodied in the Christ, was still to come; but the new era had been inaugurated in the ministry of Jesus.

In his notable book, *The Apostolic Preaching,* and again in his *The Parables of the Kingdom,* C. H. Dodd goes so far as to affirm that in the earliest form of the Christian teaching, the *kerygma,* the Death and Resurrection of Jesus Christ were held to be the final coming of the kingdom of God. So he can speak of a gospel of "realized eschatology," and he considers what he names "futuristic eschatology" to be the result of the unfortunate influence of Jewish apocalyptic. In his contention that Christian eschatology found entire fulfilment in the Ministry, the Death, and the Resurrection of Jesus, Dr. Dodd has taken too little account of the continued divine involvement in the time process, which the Incarnation means, and of the way in which from within and from beyond the process God's creative power in Christ is bringing the new into being; consequently, Dr. Dodd does not sufficiently allow for the further manifestation of that power which is yet to come. But the phrase "realized eschatology" may well stand as a forceful recognition of the truth that the career of Jesus was the beginning, in John Knox's phrase, of "a mighty eschatological event," the final issue of which is to be the consummation of the kingdom of God when he who was condemned to a malefactor's death comes in glorious majesty to exercise his lordship of the world as judge of both the quick and the dead.

It is in the light of what may be learned about the mode of the divine activity, revealed in the first coming of the King, that approach may best be made to the consideration of the character and meaning of the second coming. So, as has been noted, although it is important indeed to recognize to the full the breaking into life of the totally new in the coming of the Christ, it is just as important to keep clearly in mind that this new beginning made no denial of the achievement of the past, but was rather its fulfilment. To this, Jesus himself bore his own testimony. In the synagogue at Nazareth he read in the Scriptures from the Book of Isaiah: "The Spirit of the Lord is upon me, because he hath anointed me to preach the gospel to the poor; he hath sent me to heal the broken-hearted, to preach deliverance to the captives, and recovering of sight to the blind, to set at liberty them that are bruised, to preach the acceptable year of the Lord." And then he went on to say, "This day is this Scripture fulfilled in your ears." The divine righteousness which through all the ministry of the prophets had declared itself in behalf of the humble folk, the poor and the needy, whether by denunciation of their oppressors or by holding up before them the hope of deliverance, is here embodied in the person of One who brought first of all to the poor the good news of the kingdom and indeed identified himself with them: "Inasmuch as ye have done it unto one of the least of these my brethren, ye have done it unto me."

Again, the first two chapters of St. Luke's Gospel make vividly clear the work of the preparation for the coming of the Christ that God's disclosure of himself in Israel's history had been able to effect, as also the way in which the old could be taken up and included in the new. Zacharias and Elizabeth, Simeon and Anna, and above all the expectant mother, are there as signal reminders that the Judaism of that day is by no means to be summed up in the self-righteousness of the Pharisees or the wordliness of the priesthood. In the *Benedictus*, the *Magnificat*, and the *Nunc dimittis* the deepest longings and highest aspirations of Israel for God-given fullness of life are finding realization. The language is unmistakably that of the Old Testament, and these Christian hymns might well have their place in the Book of Psalms save for the note of intense joy in the actualization of all that the past had hoped and longed for. It is a joy for which death itself can have no terrors. Simeon's self-surrendering acceptance of the end—now that he has been given his moment of participation in God's use, through the Christ, of Israel for the salvation of a world— can hardly be paralleled in the pages of the Old Testament. The presence of the child makes all the difference, but the child was to be subject to his parents and learn from the life into which he was born that which should play its significant part in his ministry of redemption. He was "made under the law" that he might "redeem them that were under the law."

If, then, the new order inaugurated by the coming of the Christ included the fulfilment of that which God had been doing in the history of his people, the second coming for the final establishment of the kingdom may best be thought of as including a fulfilment of what God is continuing to do in this present order. There will be the new creative act; the transcendent Christ will break in upon the course of human history in final triumph. What that will mean for the time process in which human life is involved surpasses the power of conceptual thought or of the imagination. The Book of Revelation uses magnificent, if often perplexing, pictorial language—reflecting the disorders of the writer's day—to throw into sharp relief the overwhelming manifestation of power with which the Christ will come again. Theological thinking debates the question whether the end, the *telos*, is to be conceived as involving the total dissolution or, on the other hand, the transfiguration of this present world. In the light of the Incarnation—"the Word was made flesh and dwelt among us, and we beheld his glory"—it would seem that there are lasting values in our earth-bound human experience of which the proponents of a totally transcendent age to come seem hardly to take sufficient account.

As the consideration of what the second coming of the King may mean for the ordering of the kingdom fastens on the fulfilment of all that God in Christ has been doing in his world and is doing today, it is only natural to think, first of all, of the continuance of the incarnate life of our Lord in the Church. In this time of general disillusionment there are many who can think only of the failure of Christianity, and there are those who name this a post-Christian era. Indeed, it must be admitted that much that passes for religion today is but a conventional recognition of God. Even where, in what is called "the revival of religion," people do appear to be groping for something more, it seems often a kind of spiritual egoism, a simple desire for self-realization or self-integration, that would seek to use a God about whom it knows pitifully little. But granting all this, it is still true that down through the centuries millions have found in the fellowship of the Church forgiveness of sin and a glad sense of belonging to the infinite, other than self, and have discovered in this relationship a new quality of meaning for life. They have known themselves more than conquerors through him that loved them. As to the present, statistics tell, to be sure, very little; but it is well to take account of Professor K. S. Latourette's reminder that the missionary endeavor of the Christian Church is far-flung today as never before. One has only to read Bishop Newbigin's diary to take new heart from the evidence of the Church's power to bring to great numbers of simple folk new life in union with Christ. And a significant element in the life of the Church of South India is the discovery of what union with Christ means for men's union one with another, as the old ties of caste and sect are done away with. In a new setting there is realization of St. Paul's affirmation, "There is neither Jew nor Greek, there is neither bond nor free, ye are all one in Christ Jesus."

It was a Belgian monk who said that that only is to be accounted true religion that serves to bring men into union with God and so into union one with another. And Professor Paul Tillich has recently said, "Nothing is more passionately desired than social healing, than the New Being within history and human relationships"; and he adds that the signficance of the Church is that "here the reunion of man with man is pronounced and confessed and realized, even if in fragments and weakness and distortions." It is much that there is increasing awareness of the sin of disunion, that the Christian churches by whom in Dr. Tillich's phrase "the Church of God is permanently betrayed" are learning to work together as a step towards genuine unity. God is in Christ, seeking to reconcile men one to another. To recognize this in human effort is to believe that a further coming of the Christ will bring success beyond expectation, until at last in his final coming in glory the Church shall stand forth as the focus of the unity of all men in the love of God. For while to the Church has been intrusted the significant role of manifesting the joyous freedom that men may find in union with one another in Christ, it is by no means only in the Church that God in Christ is at work in his world.

(In this new age, the Christian era, the incarnate life of our Lord is affecting every aspect of human endeavor. As C. S. Lewis finely quotes, "when spring comes it leaves no corner of the earth untouched." That means that every human activity, whether of the individual or of the group, stands in an immediate relationship to God in Christ, takes place within the movement of the incarnate life which is pressing ceaselessly on to ultimate triumph. That is true not only where there is explicit acknowledgment of the worth of Christian teaching. Christ is there even when he is denied, or even where there is open antagonism.) A Friedrich Nietzsche, whose desperate longing for a more abundant life derives ultimately from Christian teaching, cannot be content until in defiance of our Lord he has written his Anti-Christ. But who shall say that the Christ would deny Nietzsche's passionate sincerity a share in his own vindication of the truth that sets men free? Or again, there is a Bernard Shaw, in W. B. Yeats' phrase "haunted by the mystery he flouts." In countless ways—amid all the striving of human beings, exercising the freedom with which God has endowed them, using or abusing the gifts and abilities which he has likewise conferred upon them—the same God in Christ is always at work. Of all the multifarious activities of man he is taking account, and in and through the play of conflicting forces he is enabling finite man to play his part in preparation for the final consummation of the kingdom.

That consummation, therefore, will include the fulfilment of all that is genuinely good in human endeavor. The greatness of the Advent Season is that it calls for the consideration of the whole process of human history. Obviously, that history includes a great deal that is not specifically religious. There is much truth in Archbishop Temple's remark that many people tend to think of God as a clergyman, and, one might add, to think of a clergyman's heaven with full attendance at all the services. But the God and Father of our Lord Jesus Christ, Creator of the ends of the earth, has not left himself without witness in any phase of man's striving; and the Advent vision of the whole must comprise the recognition of that witness in the secular as well as the religious.

So it is well to keep in mind the parallelism between religious and secular history. In the history of religion there have been long periods of unremarkable maintenance of the ordinary course of belief and practice, sustained by God's immanent activity and indeed often saved only by that activity from the deadening effect of custom. And alternating with these periods there have been times of renewal, with the breaking in of the transcendent power of God, the supreme instance of this being the coming of the King in the person of Jesus. So in secular history there has been the same alternation of the continuous and the discontinuous. There have been times of slow, gradual advance or retrogression in the ordering of life, dependent upon whether the prevailing tone has been that of use or abuse of God's giving, which has been constantly going on. And such periods have been broken in upon by the strange, the unexpected, the incalculable; and this, though it often seems bent on destruction, in the end makes in many different ways for the renewal of life. To discern within the play of these forces a coming of the transcendent creative power of the God who in Christ is participant in the human story, is to have some clear intimation of what the final coming of God in Christ will mean for the climax of that story. But the ability to discern God in the crisis will, in large measure, depend upon the way in which his power and presence have been felt in the ordinary course of events that is preparing for the crisis.

The parables of Jesus that deal with the coming of the kingdom point to the same alternation of the gradual and the catastrophic, the continuous and the discontinuous. On the one hand, it is with the kingdom as with the seed cast into the ground, that springs up and grows, man "knoweth not how: first the blade, then the ear, after that the full corn in the ear." Or again, it is as with the leaven which a woman hid in three measures of meal until the whole was leavened. Here is gradual growth or development in the fulfilment of a process continuously going on. On the other hand, in parables such as that of the wise and foolish virgins a period of waiting is, to be sure, anticipated, but the emphasis falls on the sudden, unpredictable coming of an entirely new factor. Justice can be done to both aspects of the coming only if it is remembered that the transcendent act of him who brings in the kingdom is the act of the God who in Christ is tirelessly active within and alongside of human aspiration and endeavor. It is the acknowledgment of God at work in the here and now that affords ground for the conviction that man's effort and achievement have their significant part and place in the preparation for the coming of the kingdom.

It is often said that God has come in judgment today upon a world in which selfishness, greed, and pride have taken possession of God's gifts to use them for their own ends, in utter disregard of his righteousness and love. Those whose memories go back to the early years of this century to recall the degree to which material prosperity had come to be the be-all and end-all of existence, and the smug complacency of many of those who had been able to achieve that prosperity, are bound to admit that in many ways the world was ripe for judgment. But the mode of God's judgment is all-significant. It is not as if, sitting aloof from the scene, he simply condemns man's failure to order life in accordance with standards that he has established and then sends punishment upon a hopelessly guilty world. His own loving righteousness in the incarnate life of the Christ is ceaselessly making for the good, for that which, taking account of the strange intermingling of good and evil in human decision and effort, will be for the ultimate benefit of all. This does, indeed, often involve destruction, for there is so much in the way of false pride and achievement and unreality in professed ideals that stands between man and his Maker that there come times when only a radical purging of life can allow free course for the divine creativity. God must reveal himself, in the phrase of the Epistle to the Hebrews, as "a consuming fire."

But this coming in judgment is not as some would seem to say over against all human effort and aspiration, as if man must be reduced to abject helplessness before God can find the way to enter freshly into human life. Dietrich Bonhoeffer, in his little book *Prisoner for God*, writing in what must have seemed a desperate situation, nonetheless insists more than once that God is "the beyond in the midst of life, not simply where human power gives out on the borders, but in the center of human accomplishment and joyous living." So in the present crisis God in Christ has come in judgment, but he has not come simply in condemnation; he is to be discerned also as actively present, exercising afresh his creative power in relation to all that is true and good in human effort and longing. For example, there is the awakening of the underprivileged and dispossessed in many lands to new hope of freedom from destitution, from living, as it were, on the edge of existence, to new hope of entering into fullness of life as peoples and as individuals. As peoples, for with all the evils that inhere in exaggerated nationalism there is—in the longing for the realization of the distinctive values of one's own group-life as part of the inheritance from the past and, the opportunity being given, as susceptible of rich development in the future —the evidence that the surging tide of new energy of human aspiration is not concerned merely with bread-and-butter existence but with the entering upon more abundant living as human beings. There has, of course, been preparation for this awakening in the gradual infiltration of Western ideas partly under Christian auspices and partly under auspices far from Christian; but just as it must be frankly admitted that Christian translation of its ideals into practice has fallen short, so it must be acknowledged that, even where exploitation has been ruthlessly carried on, those who have suffered this have nonetheless been learning. That is to say, in and through the confusion and cross-purposes of human activity God has been at work; and now in his own good time he comes, with new outpouring of power, to bring the world to genuine realization of the worth of every child of man in his sight and to provide new opportunity of translating that realization into the terms of all peoples' relations one with another. This, too, is a stage in that preparation which is constantly going forward for the final coming when, in the unfailing acknowledgment of the presence and power of the Christ in the glorious majesty of his righteous love, there shall be unbounded joy in the perfect reconciliation of fellowship and freedom.

In the early days of the Christian Church, so vivid was the sense of the presence of God in Christ, lifting life to new levels and endowing it with new possibilities, that it seemed as if the final triumph must be immediately at hand. But the quiet acceptance of prolonged delay, to which the New Testament itself bears witness, makes it clear that the question of the "time when" was quite a secondary one. It is not for us "to know the times and seasons." A like uncertainty must be ours as to the relation of the new order to this present world of time and space. To the question, with what body will the new age come?, the only answer can be that God will give it a body as it shall please him. In the dispensation of the fullness of time God will "gather together in one all things in Christ, both which are in heaven and which are on earth." That will surely include much that man has been striving to do, as well as what he has actually accomplished. The sharing in our human living of God in Christ endows our human activity with lasting significance. The triumph of the Christ will carry with it the triumph of a true humanism. It would seem, therefore, that means will be provided for the continuance of that creative activity in the exercise of their freedom with which God, in loving self-limitation, has endowed his children, as also for that communication one with another which is so significant a part of the creative life. In his great book, *The Incarnate Life*, Father L. S. Thornton has finely said: "The perfect social organism of the kingdom of God will include within itself the free development of all human interests and activities"; it hardly need be said that these will go on along with the constant adoring awareness of the presence of him who will still give those interests and activities their everlasting worth.

In the Advent Season, then, it is, in the first instance, "the gospel of the glory of the blessed God" that is to be delivered—the good news of a God who is living, willing, active, at work within the ordered ways of nature and in the ordinary course of events, and also disclosing himself in mighty acts (culminating in his own entrance into this life of ours for immediate redemptive participation in this our human striving, a participation which is to issue in a final triumphant vindication of his righteous love in a world subject through and through to his kingly rule)—in a word, God as revealed in the Biblical view of nature and a Biblical reading of history. It is highly significant that it should be the Collect and Epistle for the Second Sunday in Advent that dwells upon the basic importance of the Scriptures, for with all the amazing variety of the contents of the Bible— myth, legend, folklore, history, biography, poetry, the record of heroic achievement and of pitiful failure, of high aspiration and of heart-breaking despair, of corrosive scep- ticism and of burning faith—always this intensely human life is seen in its relationship to God. All the light of scholarship which has played upon its pages, bringing out in ever greater degree its wonderful variety, has only served to make more clear the marvellous unity of its unfailing reference to the divine activity. The one God is felt to be always at work in nature and in history with infinite pa- tience in his loving regard for man's freedom, both by ordered ways and by mighty transcendent acts, bringing to fulfilment his loving purpose for all his children. In the beginning, God; in the end, the world-embracing triumph of Jesus Christ. The fact of the one God, Lord of nature and of history, as the ultimate reality by whose will all lesser realities exist, is the basic truth upon which the Bibli- cal view of life as a whole is based. Against the background of this all-including truth is set the life and death and rising again of Jesus Christ, with that strange new power to desire and to love which through him streams into human life. He is the determining center of the great time process in which the living, loving God is revealing his sovereign splendor and majesty.

It is in the light of this vision of the whole, and of the certainty of the power of God in Christ at work within this present order, that the destiny of the individual is to be considered. Man's striving for good is seen as related to the incarnate life of our Lord. That is the truth that affords the ground for Christian hope. The steadfast planning and working for better things; the wisdom of leadership that will see an immediate crisis in relation to larger issues; the courage that will endure hardship to the last breath for the sake of a cause in the conviction that in the end truth and right will prevail: all these are linked with the thrusting forward of God's own energy in Christ to the fulfilment of his desire. And the strain and stress that is involved in the human struggle is to be accepted as the reminder that we are not simply spectators of the sublime movement of the divine will, but participants in it; not helplessly swept along by forces beyond our control, but able in the very ache of our striving to feel and respond to the surge of the all-conquering life of the Christ that will not be denied its ultimate triumph. By a strange paradox, that which we are really seeking—in the willing acceptance of life's discipline, with all that it involves of tension and sacrifice, and in the ability to rise above our personal desires—by these very desires, is used of God to play its part in the working out of his purpose. That which, behind all his surface wishes, a man is actually bent on—that on which his inmost desire is set, that leaning forward upon the future in the unique striving of each individual—may thus be offered to God and so, purified and transfigured, find its true fulfilment. This will inevitably come as the center of self makes loving response

to the Christ, who in the here and now is moving on to
victory. In him, in his final triumph, every soul that cares
will find the realization of all its hopes and its truest longings
and aspirations. But there is an absolute order: first of all,
a surrendering of self in the vision of the whole vast process;
and then the humble and grateful realization of one's own
part and place in it. So often the order is reversed, and
religion seems to center on a form of spiritual self-realization, with God, one might almost dare to say, playing a
useful but secondary role. It was an able Roman Catholic
who set this warning before his fellow priests: "Our efforts
have been largely salvationist. We have not tried to save
souls by building them, but by safeguarding them and
preaching religion in the terms of self-interest."

Of course, it is not to be forgotten that the phrases "for
us men and for our salvation" and "was crucified also for
us" are in the body of the Creed, but it is safe to say that
the note there is of awed wonder at the depth of the con-
descension of him who is God of God, Light of Light,
Very God of Very God. Both creeds are primarily concerned with setting forth the splendor of the divine majesty
and love, and the clauses that deal with the human situation
follow as a tremendously important kind of corollary. "We
rejoice," says St. Paul in a wonderful sentence, "we rejoice
in the hope of God's glory." Elsewhere he speaks of the
glory of God in the face of Jesus Christ. It would surely be
in accord with St. Paul's mind to think of him as rejoicing
in the hope of the glory of the Christ in his triumphant
lordship over the world in which to him every knee shall
bow. To make that hope really one's own, to care for the

consummation of our Lord's work and to live by that caring, is to feel oneself caught up in this present life into union with him, and to know that one's future is in his keeping.

He to whom the future can thus be committed is no unknown being. It is the conviction that, as the limited little self is immersed in and penetrated by the measureless unfailing flow of energy that the constant onward movement of life represents, it is being carried along from moment to moment by the untiring activity of God himself; and that within this streaming life the love of God in Christ is constantly pressing in upon us, claiming it for its own—it is this conviction that issues in the glowing certainty of a life beyond the grave. Yielding self brings a sense of belonging to the God of all power and love, a feeling, therefore, of release from the hold of past failures and sins and of abounding vitality that, because it draws upon a source beyond self, is capable of dealing quietly and effectively with the day-by-day problems and difficulties with which it is confronted in times of perplexity and struggle. It is not the sense of hopeless frustration in this life that, as is sometimes said, gives rise to a full-bodied belief in the life to come. That belief springs rather from a realization of the tremendous worthwhileness of life as it is lived in this world, knowing here and now the power of our Lord's Resurrection and the fellowship of his sufferings, being made conformable unto his death—the death of him whose cry, "Father, into thy hands I commend my spirit," followed upon a lifetime of loving response to the Father's will in all the circumstances of daily living.

After death the judgment: to turn to the consideration of this is to think of the kind of being man is as capable of response to the will of God. Man can choose; he is endowed with freedom. It is perhaps not surprising that for many people that great word still means little more than absence of restraint. It was Abraham Lincoln who said that the world has never had a good definition of liberty. It may be that this is because liberty is so related to the very springs of life that like life itself it baffles definition. And so the tendency is to dwell upon the removal of obstacles—social, economic, political. It is indeed necessary to do this because conditions so often impose a kind of slavery upon great numbers of people. But freedom that is not thought of as a mere negative, a pointless roaming in an empty world, looks beyond itself. It is the ability of the individual to make his own distinctive, creative response to life, the response of his unique, irreplaceable individuality. In giving him the ability to make this response, God has conferred upon the individual a measure of independence as over against himself.

Again, it is the doctrine of God that is of primary importance. His creative power and love are supremely manifest in his bestowal of independence on his creatures. On this point it is interesting to see the able Jesuit theologian Erich Przywara quoting Kierkegaard: "God's omnipotence is shown in His love, for love gives of itself entirely, but in such a way as gradually to withdraw itself and let the object of one's love be independent. Only omnipotent power can thus confer independence, bringing forth out of nothing that which has its own power of existence." That is the amazing truth—that God gives, continues to give of his own sustaining creative energy, while leaving the individual free to make or fail to make creative use of his gift. A man is therefore a center of becoming, and at his very core he is shaping himself by his choices. Every actual choice becomes part of a record—a record imprinted deep in his own being—of far greater consequence than any which others may scan with approval or disapproval, for it is the indelible record of the self that he is becoming as in thought and word and deed he makes his distinctive response to the varied demands and opportunities with which life faces him. "Each one of us shall give account of himself to God." It is unfortunate that for so many people the divine judgment is thought of as dependent upon a kind of celestial bookkeeping by which it is determined whether there is a balance of good or evil deeds in each individual life. The real accounting which each must finally give of himself is the kind of person he has become in the day-by-day exercise of his God-given freedom.

Perhaps it may be said without too much exaggeration that for the individual the hope of the future both here and hereafter lies upon the continuance of the capacity for exercising that freedom. It is indeed God's gift, but it is only in the grateful acknowledgment of the Giver, the acknowledgment of his presence and power in the life within and around us, and in the constant effort to discern and obey the promptings of his love that the capacity for freedom—that is, for the creative response to life—can be retained and developed. It is only too easy to make self the center and so seek to appropriate out of life all about us what may seem to be to our advantage. In the realm of morals, honest thinking in any given situation is aware of the subtle power of the instinct to let self-interest dictate decisions. But at the same time we may still be quite oblivious of the way in which self-centeredness may pervade our total attitude, determining again and again the response that we make to life's impact upon us. In the appreciation of beauty, for example, it is possible to be content with the hasty recognition of just so much in it as gives us an immediate satisfaction, and fail, therefore, to see it as, so to speak, having a life of its own that calls for the effort to understand what it is trying to say to us. And so we miss the glimpse of his own glory that God is offering. Or again, in the exercise of the mind there can be a passive contentment with just so much of truth as may seem serviceable, as can be comprised perhaps in some formula, or as can fall in with preconceived theory. And so there is little of the sense of responsibility before God to use to the full all the powers of understanding that he has given us, with a resultant failure to feel the depth upon depth of reality in which there is always the something more that claims us for its service.

This self-centeredness, often half unconscious, brings, if persisted in, a habit of seeing life all about one, the life of others, even the life of God himself, only as it can be measured by one's own interests; and as the years go by there ensues, strangely enough, a steady narrowing of those interests and of one's outlook upon the world. The self seems to become more and more important, as the only thing that has reality, while any apparent reason for its worth becomes less and less, shut up as it increasingly is in the prison house of its own desires and appetites. As one of the characters in T. S. Eliot's *The Cocktail Party* puts it:

> Hell is oneself,
> Hell is alone, the other figures in it
> Merely projections. There is nothing to escape from
> And nothing to escape to: One is always alone. (Act I,
>   Scene 3)[1]

That which saves man from this final loneliness is the continuous effort to respond in his life here to the presence of God as he seeks to make himself known in the circumstances of daily living, as also in the times of especial illumination that in his mercy he grants to us all.

Again, it is the doctrine of God that is all-important. He is Personal Being, and in making response to him, whether in adoration or in loving obedience to his will in the daily round, all that is most deeply personal in the self is called forth. As can be seen in human friendship at its best, the I-Thou relationship is reciprocal. In union with God's creative activity, our own power of creative response is enhanced; and with our own sense of renewed and deepened contact with reality there comes new power of discernment of the God-given reality in the life of others. But more than that, it is God in Christ who makes himself known in our inner life and in the world all about us. In life's strain and stress, too, we are drawn into closer union with One who accepted it all, even to a death upon the cross. "I am crucified with Christ; nevertheless I live. Yet not I, but Christ

---

[1] New York: Harcourt, Brace and Company, Inc., 1950; London: Faber and Faber, 1950.

liveth in me." And the same Christ is to be seen in the lives of others, it may be, governing them or, it may be, striving to overcome indifference, ignorance, or defiance. "Christ in hearts of all that love me, Christ in mouth of friend and stranger." To make response to his presence in all the contacts, opportunities, and demands that life affords is to have an ever-deepening sense of the mystery and wonder of God's world and increasingly loving insight into the reality of the lives of those about us as we go on learning to live in the largeness of God's love. Aware of our Lord's coming and coming again into our life and into the lives of others, it will seem inevitable that the day will dawn when, in the presence of his glorious majesty, instead of a partial, intermittent obedience there will be unfailing response to his love in all that men do and are. And the consummation of his victory will mean, to his joy, the realization to the full of the glorious liberty of the children of God.

CHAPTER TWO

Preaching in Christmastide
and the Epiphany Season

BY ALBERT T. MOLLEGEN

UNDERSTANDING THE CHURCH YEAR

THE CHURCH YEAR, like the New Testament, arose within the Church. Neither the Church Year nor the New Testament is therefore to be taken as speaking about any holy event except in the light of the all-determining holy events, the Resurrection of Christ and the Communication of the Holy Spirit. The early Church *Pascha* was a *Resurrection* festival and this fact finally placed the Easter Eucharist *at dawn on Sunday*. It is more than probable that the quartodeciman use of the Asian churches differed from the rest of the Church *only* in the matter of dating the *Pascha*, not in any failure to include as its climax the Resurrection. As A. Allan McArthur writes: "Asia took a different starting-point from the Church as a whole, and it may be said, simply as a statement of fact, that Asia began from the Passion whereas the other churches began from the Resurrection. But it cannot be said that the different starting points controlled the whole nature of the festival. Rather, the evidence suggests that everywhere the *Pascha*, a unitive commemoration, moved through the austerity of the vigil and the memorial of the Cross to the end of the fast and the glory of the Triumph. The difference consisted, not in the nature of the liturgical celebration, but in the mode of the liturgical calculation." [1]

Pentecost probably originally celebrated the Ascension as well as the coming of the Spirit so that the whole period of fifty days from Easter to Pentecost was a festival time in which both fasting and kneeling were forbidden as they were on the Lord's Day, i.e., every Sunday. Tertullian, for instance, writes: "We count fasting or kneeling in worship on the Lord's day to be unlawful. We rejoice in the same privilege also from Easter to Whitsunday." [2]

It would seem, therefore, that the history of the development of the Church Year shows clearly what all Christians know religiously and theologically—that Easter-Whitsunday, Resurrection and the Communication of the Holy Spirit, determine the whole character of the Church Year. Easter-Whitsunday, then, create Christmas and Epiphany as well as the other seasons of the Church Year. It is the Easter-Ascension-Whitsunday revelation which transforms the bad Friday of Jesus' Crucifixion into the Good Friday of the Christian Church Year. It was the *Lord* who is at the right hand of God and who pours out the Holy Spirit upon us, who was crucified for us, so that it is a *Good* Friday.

[1] *The Evolution of the Christian Year* (Greenwich: The Seabury Press, 1955), p. 102. (London: Student Christian Movement Press, Ltd.)
[2] Quoted by McArthur, *ibid.*, p. 148. McArthur documents this practice not only from Tertullian but also from Canon 20 of the Council of Nicaea, Cassian, Origen, Athanasius, Basil and Augustine, *ibid.*, pp. 148-9.

Every aspect of the Church Year must therefore be preached from within the Community of the Holy Spirit in communion with the Ascended Lord, who is recognized and honored as himself. Easter-Whitsunday creates for us the Christian meaning of the birth of Jesus and of his manifestation to the simple Jews (the Shepherds) and the wise Gentiles (the Magi).

Everywhere it is the whole Christ in his whole revelation of himself who deals with us in the Church Year. It is Christ who came, ministered, was crucified, is risen, is ascended, and who breathes out his Spirit upon us—it is this, the only Christ, whose nativity is celebrated in Christmastide as a birth for us. It is this, the only Christ, whose manifestation to us and the world is celebrated during the Epiphany season. It is this Christ whose earthly life conforms us to itself in Lent, whose Death-Resurrection was for us and is received by us in Baptism in the Good Friday-Easter period leading us into the Easter Eucharist, whose Ascension we share here and now as an earnest (*arrabon*, first-installment) of the life which we shall have in fulness at his second Advent. Because he has given us his Spirit (Whitsunday), he has enabled us to share his life and live that life by and with him.

Since this is true, our preaching can never retreat behind the Easter-Whitsunday season, either chronologically or in spirit, except as a way of showing the world's blindness to the Christ whom we see and serve as the Lord and the Spirit-giver. Preaching the Church Year does not intend or seek an act of the historical imagination which reproduces the life of Jesus unrecognized as the Ascended Lord. Inso-

much as we preach the events of Christmas through Good
Friday as pre-Whitsunday events, we preach no Christian
Gospel at all. Insomuch as we preach these events as part
of the Gospel, we preach Christ the Lord in his humble
coming and his non-coercive manifestation.

This may be put in another way. Participation in the
Holy Spirit is participation in the life of Christ at the right
hand of God. It is eschatology in the process of being ac-
tualized in history as our holy history, sacred history, sanctified history. Every event commemorated in the Church
Year, therefore, participates in eschatological time, time
filled up with divine meaning and divine living. Preaching
cannot permit these historical events to fall out of participation in eschatological time. For example, the glory of the
eschatological age must permeate and shine through the
historical time of Advent. The Advent Season is the Old
Testament time eagerly expecting the coming of the Messiah and the Messianic age; it is our Church Militant time
eagerly expecting the Second Coming of our Lord and the
Christian Consummation.

In possessing historical events only as they participate in
eschatological time, the Church Year is true to the New
Testament. For not a word or an event of the New Testament is preserved except as it partakes of the eternal age
which is to come. In the Gospels, every word of Jesus and
every deed which he does or suffers is recorded because he
is the Lord of the eschatological kingdom, recognized as
such in the Resurrection. St. John, for example, narrates the
entry of Jesus into Jerusalem. The crowd greets Jesus by
quoting from the 118th Psalm and St. John sees the event as

fulfilling the prophecy of Zechariah 9:9, "Fear not, daughter of Zion; behold thy King is coming, sitting on an ass's
colt!" St. John then says quite clearly that neither the
relation of the entry into Jerusalem to Scripture nor its
significance as an event was understood until Jesus' Crucifixion, Resurrection and Ascension, that is, until Christ's
glorification. St. John wrote: "His disciples did not understand this at first; but when Jesus was glorified, then they
remembered that this had been written of him and had been
done to him" (Jn. 12:16). The glorification of Jesus gave
us the true meaning of his entry into Jerusalem and so also
his glorification gave us the true meaning of all of his words
and deeds. All of the Gospels so present his earthly speaking
and acting. One illustration of this may be given from St.
Mark's Gospel. In that Gospel, the Church (the readers and
hearers of St. Mark's Gospel) knows from the beginning
who Jesus is. We hear the divine voice address him at his
baptism as "My beloved Son"; we know that at his baptism
the heavens opened and the Spirit descended upon him
(Mk. 1:9-11). We are inside "the mystery of the Kingdom
of God" (Mk. 4:11). But it is not until the Transfiguration
that the insiders of Jesus' time, Peter, James and John, begin
darkly and confusedly to understand who Jesus is. The
divine voice says to *them* at the Transfiguration what Jesus
and we have heard at the Baptism of Jesus, "This is my
beloved Son; listen to him" (Mk. 9:7). But Jesus charges
the inner three not to tell what they have seen "until the
Son of Man should have risen from the dead" (Mk. 9:9).
The three immediately demonstrate the wisdom of Jesus'
command, for as they obey it they reveal why they should

obey it. They do not understand the Resurrection. "So they kept the matter [of the Transfiguration] to themselves, questioning what the rising from the dead meant" (Mk. 9:10). Not until the Resurrection did Peter, James and John understand the true meaning of the Transfiguration or of anything else that Jesus said, did or suffered.

Our point is simple. The Church Year is a continual *anamnesis* of the sacred events in which the whole Christ comes to us and draws us into participation in him. The Church Year draws our life into Christ's life, our time into eschatological time, our *chronos* into God's *kairos*. The Church Year is the Bible represented in our time for us, continuing the sacred history that both participates in and expects the Consummation of all things.

Anamnesis does not mean that by an act of the historical imagination we go out of our time into past time—say, from the twentieth to the first century. *Anamnesis* means that we call the revelatory events of the past time into our present to form, shape, give meaning to the contemporary meeting with God. We meet now in our time the Jesus who is the Christ who was made manifest in the flesh in the first century. And we meet him as he who is to come in majesty and glory to judge the quick and the dead. Thus, in the Advent collect we ask grace to enter deeper into our Baptism, to "cast away the works of darkness, and put upon us the armour of light" which the Epistle defines clearly: "But put ye on the Lord Jesus Christ, and make not provision for the flesh." The Lord Jesus can be put on by us because he has taken our flesh unto himself. This "now in the time of this mortal life" is that in which God's Son

"Jesus Christ came to visit us in great humility," the great humility of the Incarnation. And this "putting on the Lord Jesus" is the here and now first-installment of our rising "to the life immortal" in the last day "when he shall come again." Only by understanding liturgical time as historical time filled with eschatological time can we understand why the Triumphal Entry into Jerusalem, as recorded by St. Matthew, can be the Gospel for the First Sunday in Advent while St. Matthew's narrative of the trial of Jesus before Pilate and of Jesus' Crucifixion is the Gospel for Palm Sunday. Neither the first Sunday in Advent nor Palm Sunday takes us back of the first Easter and the first Whitsunday. The first Sunday in Advent calls us to be clothed with him who has come in the first century, who continually comes to his world to claim it as his Jerusalem and to cleanse his temple, and who will come finally to claim his creation and to purify his Church completely. Advent is not different from Palm Sunday in historical time as John the Baptist's preaching is different in historical time from the Triumphal Entry. Advent is the Triumphal Entry received as *preparation* for Christ's coming. Palm Sunday, as its Epistle tells us, is the Triumphal Coming of Christ to become "obedient unto death, even the death of the cross" and to be exalted in the eyes of faith to that which he truly is and which the whole universe will confess in the end, "Jesus Christ is Lord, to the glory of God the Father." But Palm Sunday is this triumphal coming not to prepare us for Christ's first coming but to lead us through the Trial, Crucifixion, Resurrection and the centurion's confession into imitation of his humility. As the Palm Sunday Collect says,

Christ came and was crucified "that all mankind should follow the example of his great humility." We to whom he is "our Saviour" therefore pray "that we may both follow the example of his patience, and also be made partakers of his resurrection." Advent is preparation for Christ's continual and Second Coming, Holy Week is actualization in us of his coming. But this difference is only in accent, for we prepare by actualizing, "putting on the armor of light," and we actualize by preparing, by praying, "Mercifully grant, that we . . . may both follow . . . and also be made partakers."

All of this should not be understood as great and deliberate subtlety on the part of the Church. It is far from this. Almost any "coming" of Christ in the New Testament would suffice for the Advent and Palm Sunday Gospels although not many would do as well. Not subtlety but massive, rough-hewn, elemental experience of Christ informs the mind of the Church as it expresses itself in the Church Year. Informed by the New Testament and tradition, the Church may well improve the Church Year, the seasonal collects and the choice of Biblical passages to be read, but the great accents should always be kept and should inform our preaching of the seasons.

CHRISTMASTIDE AND THE EPIPHANY SEASON

The accent of Advent is preparation for the coming of Christ on the basis of his first coming. The accent of Christmastide is the *receiving* of Christ on the basis of his having come. Christmastide therefore shows forth the great dialectical relation of the expectation of and the reception of

Christ. This event, the taking of our nature upon him by the only-begotten Son of God, splits history into two segments.

Christmas divides history into B. C. history and A. D. history, history before Christ and history which is constituted as the years of our Lord. B. C. history, however, is seen as the original Advent Season only when it is seen in the light of the coming of Christ. Christmas celebrates the coming of the whole Christ, he who came, ministered, was crucified, was raised, communicated his Spirit, still comes and will come in the last day. It was this Christ who was being prepared for in Old Testament history and in pagan history, but this is seen only with the coming of Christ. Judaism's preparation for the Messiah does not understand itself as preparation for Jesus as the Messiah until Jesus has come. To receive Jesus as the Christ is also at the same time to receive the true meaning of the Old Testament. This is said clearly, frequently, and in many ways in the New Testament. In St. Luke, Cleopas and his companion at the Emmaus supper recognize the Risen Jesus "in the breaking of the bread" and exclaim, "Did not our hearts burn within us while he talked to us on the road, *while he opened to us the scriptures*" (Lk. 24:32). And in a later resurrection appearance St. Luke reports, "Then he opened their minds *to understand the scriptures*" (24:45). Christ, said St. Paul, was the seed (singular number) promised by God to Abraham (Gal. 3:16).

Still again, the Johannine Christ makes acceptance of himself the test by which the Jews show that they are children of Abraham. Rejection of Christ shows them to be children of the devil, not of God or of Abraham. Christ, therefore, is the hidden depth of Old Testament expectation. "Your father Abraham rejoiced that he was to see my day; he saw it and was glad" (Jn. 8:56). The Eternal Son of God who is incarnate as Jesus of Nazareth was seen in his kingship and in his Kingdom yet to come by Abraham. "Truly, truly, I say to you, before Abraham was, I am" (Jn. 8:58). This is the theological truth that underlies all typology.

But Christ in his historical manifestation also discloses himself as the unrecognized depth of all pagan expectation. He came as St. Paul said, *to the Jew first, and also to the Greek*. This gives us our primary Christmas-Epiphany theme. The Incarnation is the Coming and Manifestation of Christ first among the Jews, then among the Gentiles, the non-Jews. The dialectical relation of prepared-expectation to reception, of Christmas to B. C. time, unveils B. C. time as really Advent Season time. But this unveiling is a part of the rending of the Temple veil, the price of which is Christ's Passion. In St. Mark's Gospel the expulsion of Jesus' last breath (*exepneusen*), the rending of the veil when God moves out of the Jewish holy of holies, and the *Gentile* centurion's confession are in immediate conjunction.

> And Jesus uttered a loud cry, and breathed his last. And the curtain of the temple was torn in two, from top to bottom. And when the centurion, who stood facing him, saw that he thus breathed his last (*exepneusen*), he said, 'Truly this man was a Son of God' (Mk. 15:37–39).

The Passion and Death of Christ not only is the breaking forth of God from the Holy of Holies in the Jewish Temple, the rending of the veil which separated God from the people. The Passion and Death of Christ also makes Gentiles' reception of him possible.

The Cross, therefore, stands between Judaism and Christianity. Christianity sees Judaism through the Cross as the divine preparation for Christ. Old Testament history is seen as the original Advent Season. But Judaism as the preparation for Christ is not the Judaism which crucifies Christ and sees the Cross as a stumbling block. Old Testament history as the first Advent Season is not the Old Testament history which the Jews understand. Christ's death exposes Judaism's false expectation even as Christ risen unveils and fulfils Judaism's true expectation. On Christmas Day we celebrate the Eucharist which makes *anamnesis* of Christ's Death and Resurrection for us. We celebrate the birth of Christ who has died and been raised for us. Christmas, therefore, reveals Old Testament time as the original Advent Season.

This same motif moves onward to the Gentiles, the pagans. Christmas, with its Eucharist which includes *anamnesis* of the Cross and Resurrection, unveils the depth of pagan expectation as expectation of Jesus as the Christ. For Christianity sees and understands paganism through the Cross *and Judaism.* This is why the Church carries not only Christ but also the Old Testament to the Gentiles. But paganism seen through Christ and the Old Testament is not the paganism which sees the Cross as foolishness and the Old Testament as narrow particularism. Christ, in his Old Testament context, reveals paganism's true expectation, even as he fulfils that expectation.

Judaism understood its need as the need to become worthy to receive vindication from God. Its real need was for forgiveness and humble service to the Gentile. So also paganism must reunderstand itself. Paganism understood its need as the need for divine immortality. Its real need was for deliverance from sin and resurrection in Christ. Gentiles who understood the human problem as mortality had to understand that problem in a deeper way. The human problem is sin, and death is the wages of that sin. And only through "the Law" comes the knowledge of sin. The Gentiles, therefore, like St. Mark's Syrophoenician woman who sought Christ for exorcism for her daughter, may receive Christ's benefits only when they understand those benefits as coming to the (Gentile) dogs from the (Jewish) children's table. Not only Christ but the Christian understanding of the Old Testament is the Gentile's necessary preparation.

The Prologue to the Fourth Gospel, originally chosen as the Gospel for the third and last Christmas Mass, seems the perfect choice for the Christmas Gospel. It was chosen in the West for a Christmas Gospel before Advent Season arose so that Christmas began the Church Year. The Eastern Churches have it as their Easter Gospel because Easter begins their Church Year. The rise of the Advent Season in no wise changes this meaning of beginning the Christian time, for, as we have seen, Christmas gives us the true meaning of pre-Christian history, Jewish and pagan. The Johannine Prologue must be interpreted on Christmas Day in its liturgical context, whatever may be its exegesis in terms of historical criticism. We may begin the liturgical exegesis with the final sentence, "And the Word was made flesh, and dwelt among us, (and we beheld his glory, the glory as of the only begotten of the Father,) full of grace and truth." Jesus, the visible, audible, tangible historical man was the eternal Word of God. "It is through a knowledge of this [Jesus'] life that the Eternal Logos is apprehended, and not otherwise." [3]

Moving backward through the Prologue, the Word made flesh, Jesus, came unto his own, the Jews, and the Jews received him not; but as many as received him, to them he gave the power to become sons of God. These receiving ones are those who "believe on his name" and are baptized. They are born of water and the Spirit, not of man but of God, "not of blood, nor of the will of the flesh, nor of the will of man, but of God." Thus, as Jesus among the Jews, the Word was the true light "which lighteth every man that cometh into the world." He was witnessed to by John the Baptist, he was the Light shining in the darkness of Jewish unbelief and not overcome by it. Read this way, everything from the fifth verse may be understood of the historic career of Jesus. Perhaps even verse four, "In him was life; and the life was the light of men," may also speak of Jesus as the Incarnate Word communicating to Christians the Eternal Life which is in him. Only the first three verses from this standpoint refer to the pre-existent, unincarnate Logos. But, as we have seen, this Jesus set forth by the Church Year is the fulfilment of the deep and true expectation of both Jew and Gentile. The history of Jesus, the Word made flesh, is, therefore, the concrete and effective actualization of the Logos' relationship to all human history, Jewish and Gentile, and to the Creation itself. For

[3] C. H. Dodd, *The Interpretation of the Fourth Gospel* (New York: Cambridge University Press, 1953), p. 284.

the Word made flesh unveiling and fulfilling the deepest need of Jew and Gentile is the Word who was in the beginning, who was God, by whom all things were made. The logos of the creation, the image of the Divine Logos, receives from the Divine Logos its existence and its power to resist non-existence, its light which is not overcome or comprehended by darkness. The Divine Logos before his Incarnation has been enlightening every man, has been coming unreceived and partially received by his own, his creation and his human creatures.

And this interpretation may well be the right historical exegesis of the Prologue to the Fourth Gospel. C. H. Dodd, facing the problem of when the author of St. John's Gospel begins to speak of the historic Jesus, whether it is at verse 11 or at verse 4 or at some verse between, writes: ". . . I suggest that the true solution of the problem may be found if we take with the fullest seriousness the implication of the proposition, *ho logos sarx egeneto*, in the light of the whole story that follows. The Logos did not merely descend upon Jesus, enter into Him, or abide in Him. The Logos *became* the *sarx* or human nature which He bore. The life of Jesus therefore *is* the history of the Logos as incarnate, and this must be, upon the stage of limited time, the same thing as the history of the Logos in perpetual relations with man and the world. Thus not only verses 11–13, but the whole passage from verse 4, is *at once* an account of the relations of the Logos with the world, *and* an account of the ministry of Jesus Christ, which in every essential particular reproduces those relations." [4]

Dodd's statement that "the ministry of Jesus Christ . . .

[4] *Ibid.*, pp. 283–4.

in every essential particular reproduces" the relations of the Logos with the World must not be taken as final, for the Christmas Gospel liturgically understood and the Prologue of the Fourth Gospel certainly mean that the Logos as Jesus, not only reproduces the perpetual relations of the Logos with the world, but *actualizes* for the first time a relationship which God intended from the beginning and for which Jewish and pagan man thirsted from the beginning. But the thirst does not understand itself as thirst for Jesus Christ until Jesus comes and is received as the Christ. This points us toward an Epiphany Season Gospel, the story of the Wedding at Cana, where man's thirst is met not by the Jewish waters of purification nor by the Dionysian wine made from water, but by Christ's wine, his blood poured out on Calvary and drunk in the Christian Eucharist.

Christ was born among the *Jews* and the Church celebrates his birth on the winter-solstice, the *pagan* "Birthday of the Sun-God." Christmas unveils and fulfils the deepest need and the true expectation of Jew and pagan.

THE THREE WITNESS DAYS

Christmas Day is followed by the commemoration of St. Stephen's martyrdom. Whatever may have been the relationship of these two days originally, it was inevitable that they should quickly be bound together in meaning as well as in time. The Epistle emphasizes St. Stephen's conformity to our Lord's death in that he dies filled with the Holy Ghost, seeing the Son of Man on the right hand of God and with forgiveness for his slayers. The Church's first martyr is commemorated on the day following the commemoration of our Lord's Nativity, the beginning of the New Age. So also St. John's and Holy Innocents' Days become a part of a pattern which has many variations in the history of the Church's preaching. St. Stephen is a martyr both in will and deed. St. John is a martyr in will but not in deed. The Holy Innocents are martyrs in deed but not yet in will. All Christians are encompassed by these three types of martyrs. St. Stephen is a conscious witness to Christ whose witness precipitates a martyr's premature death. St. John, a conscious witness to Christ, according to a tradition as old as the twenty-first chapter of St. John's Gospel, lived an extraordinarily long life. The Holy Innocents, not conscious witnesses to Christ, died very prematurely at the age of two years or younger.

Massey Shepherd's comment on St. John's Day Gospel will suffice for St. Stephen's and St. John's Days. John 21:19ff., he writes, "has been a source of two traditions: the martyrdom of St. Peter and the long life of the Apostle John. Whatever may be the historical truth of these traditions, the important lesson of this Gospel is that discipleship means following Christ regardless of what temporal fate may await us." [5] But Holy Innocents' Day has need for further exposition for three reasons. First the Holy Innocents were innocent. In the Middle Ages they were identified with the 144,000 in the Day's Epistle. Singing a new song before God, a song which no others could learn, "these were they which were not defiled with women; for they are virgins. These are they which follow the Lamb

[5] Massey H. Shepherd, *The Oxford American Prayer Book Commentary* (New York: Oxford University Press, 1950), pp. 101–2.

whithersoever he goeth. These were redeemed from among men, being the first-fruits unto God and to the Lamb" (Rev. 14:4). Holy Innocents' Day, with or without the Medieval understanding, confronts us with the mystery of innocence and of the inseparability of sin and experience. Kiddle, in his Moffatt commentary on the Epistle, quotes a passage from John Donne's Devotions:

> The soul of sin (for we have made sin immortal), the soul of sin is disobedience to thee; and when one sin hath been dead in me, that soul hath passed into another sin. Our youth dies, and the sins of our youth with it; some sins die a violent death, and some a natural; poverty, penury, imprisonment, banishment, kill some sins in us, and some die of old age; many ways we become unable to do that sin, but still the soul (i.e. the soul of sin) lives and passes into another sin; and that that was licentiousness becomes ambition, and that comes to indevotion and spiritual coldness; we have three lives in our state of sin, and where the sins of our youth expire, those of our middle years enter, and those of our age after them. This transmigration of sin in me, makes me afraid, O my God, of a relapse. . . .

No one who approves this as a description of human experience can also reject the appreciation of innocence at the price of experience. Infants may be entrusted to God as premature martyrs who fell in the battle with man's last enemy, death. The Church understands their early deaths as martyrdoms, for it, by faith, takes their deaths into union with Christ's death. And the Church understands their innocency as a blessing that maturity could scarcely have achieved. On Holy Innocents' Day, the Liturgy commemorates the children's deaths as martyrdoms and holds their innocency before us as something to be maintained in us by grace "even unto death."

The Gospel shows us a strategy in maintaining innocency which we may learn from our Lord's Infancy. The Holy Family fled the enmity of Herod the Great at God's command to Joseph, "Arise, and take the young child and his mother, and flee into Egypt, and be thou there until I bring thee word: for Herod will seek the young child to destroy him" (The Day's Gospel). The innocency of our Lord was not maintained by a foolhardy strategy which defied the power of this world before he was strong enough to face it. He fled the inimical power of Herod, and later the inimical power of Archelaus until he was mature enough to face and overcome the powers of this world. Egypt and Nazareth, the synagogue, the Temple and the Holy Family, were used by God to nurture Christ's manhood into the strong instrument of his Deity which is seen in his ministry and in Gethsemane. American eagerness to act is judged by our Lord's long preparation for his ministry, and the coming season of Lent is pointed to as our withdrawal from the world to be conformed to Israel's forty years' preparation in the wilderness and our Lord's forty days alone with God and Satan. The Christ who is formed in us by Baptismal Grace is to be nurtured in the Family of God in which he dwells as Holy Spirit, in the Body of Christ which is the Church which is maturing into the mature man which it shall be in the last day.

The second reason for attention to Holy Innocents' Day is that the Holy Innocents are infants, that is, immature. Implied in accepting them as martyrs is the Church's affirmation of their maturation beyond death. Their martyrdom may become a martyrdom in will as well as in deed. The power of Christ over death is a power which overcomes the consequences of premature death. Dead infants grow to maturity in Christ before the Great Consummation. Two prayers from the Service for Burial of a Child continue the above two themes of Holy Innocents' Day, innocency as a norm for us and children's maturation beyond death.

> Almighty and merciful Father, who dost grant to children an abundant entrance into thy kingdom; Grant us grace so to conform our lives to their innocency and perfect faith, that at length, united with them, we may stand in thy presence in fulness of joy; through Jesus Christ our Lord. Amen.
>
> O merciful Father, whose face the angels of thy little ones do always behold in heaven; Grant us stedfastly to believe that this thy child hath been taken into the safe keeping of thine eternal love; through Jesus Christ our Lord. Amen.

Thirdly, the Holy Innocents were unbaptized Jews. If their martyrdom is accounted for them as their baptism, their martyrdom is in deed and not yet in will. This raises for us the whole problem of invincible ignorance in respect to faith. Although Anglicanism has no dogma in respect to this problem, it seems clear that its general position has been that the limbo of unbaptized infants is not in accord with the Gospel and that there is no final limbo for anyone. This means that for those who are invincibly ignorant there shall be the opportunity to accept Christ. Two dogmas are thus protected. First, the dogma of God's justice. Participation in the Consummation will not be denied to anyone for not having that which he has had no opportunity to have. Second, faith in Christ and membership in his body, the Church, is the only access to the Consummation. *Extra ecclesiam nulla salus* is true eschatologically.

THE UNITY OF CHRISTMAS AND EPIPHANY

It is clear that Christmas and Epiphany were not originally separated as Festivals of the Birth and of the Manifestation of Christ. Probably they developed as separate unitive festivals of Birth-Manifestation on different dates, Epiphany in the East and Christmas in Rome. The acceptance by Rome of Epiphany on January sixth with its commemoration of the visit of the Magi gave it the character of "The Manifestation to the Gentiles" suggesting the Christmastide as a manifestation to the Jews. As we have seen, however, the new light of the incarnate Word came to the Jew that it might come to the Gentiles also, so that manifestation to *mankind* is contained in the Christmastide propers. The Christmas Collect's petition is that we "may daily be renewed by thy Holy Spirit" but this daily renewal comes to the regenerate who are made children of God by adoption and grace, that is by our rebirth, baptism by water and the Spirit, given to us by Christ as we receive him, believe on his name. God gives us his only-begotten Son to take our nature upon him and to be born man that we might be reborn as children of God. On Christmas, at one and the same time we rejoice in the incredible birth of the Son among us and in our incredible rebirth. For these are great miracles. In the Gospel of St. Mark, when Jesus has said that it is easier for a camel to go through the eye of a needle than for a rich man to enter the kingdom of God, the disciples are astonished and ask, "Then who can be saved?" Jesus' reply is, "With men it is impossible, but not with God; for all things are possible with God" (Mk. 10:26-27). Our rebirth and renewal daily by the Holy Spirit is not a human possibility but a divine work. "See what love the Father has given us, that we should be called children of God; and so we are," wrote St. John in his First Epistle. This miracle of being made children of God is further elaborated in the Epistle for the First Sunday after Christmas. This Epistle, which is from the fourth chapter of Galatians, may be paraphrased as follows:

A child is put under tutors and governors by his father until the appointed time for him to enter into his sonship. Though the child is in principle heir and lord, he is no different from a slave, he is under masters. Even so, before Christ we Christians (Jews and Gentiles) were slaves to the demonic powers of this world. But at the time appointed of the Father, God sent forth his Son, born of a woman (he was a man), born under the Law (he was a Jew), to redeem them that were under the Law (the Jews) in order that we (Christians who were Jews and Gentiles) might receive the adoption of sons.

The whole understanding of this Epistle lies in what St. Paul means by "the fulness of the time." Obviously, it means the time when the Jews had been prepared for the coming of Christ. Because the Jews were prepared the world was prepared. The Jews were the Son's point of entry into the world as the Incarnate Son. What, according to St. Paul, was the essence of this preparation? From the analogy of the Roman father, son, tutors and governors, preparation consists in maturation under physical, mental, and moral disciplines. But what is the religious counterpart of this education according to St. Paul? The seventh chapter of Romans is the answer. Maturity that is ready for Christ's coming is man's despair under the Law, the confession of tragic impotence, the cry for a deliverer. And St. Paul rightly interprets Judaistic history, for the clearer the revelation of God became, the greater was Judaism's understanding of the alienation of the world from God. This is one of the central themes of Jewish Apocalyptic. As (Fourth) Ezra said to the angel after he had surveyed the history of revelation and his people:

> For what profit is it for all that are in this present time to live in heaviness, and after death to look for punishment? O thou Adam, what hast thou done? for though it was thou that sinned, the evil is not fallen on thee alone, but upon all of us that come of thee. For what profit is it unto us, if there be promised us an immortal time, whereas we have done the works that bring death?—And that there shall be shewed a paradise, whose fruit endureth without decay, wherein is abundance and healing, but we shall not enter into it, for we have walked in unpleasant places? (II Esdras 7:47-54)

The angel's answer is that only a very few will be saved including Ezra. It is part of the dialectical relation of Judaism and Christianity that St. Paul should at once deny even to the few salvation by the Law and open to all, even to the Gentiles, outside the Law, justification by God's Act in Christ received by the response of faith. The preparation for Christ's coming, as St. Paul understood it, was to know that "the very commandment which promised life proved to be death to me" (Rom. 7:10). And no "few" escaped by their obedience. "For no human being will be justified in his [God's] sight by works of the law since through the law comes knowledge of sin" (Rom. 3:20). The predicament is universal, ". . . all men, both Jews and Greeks, are under the power of sin" (3:9). The fulness of time therefore, for St. Paul, centered in man's awareness of his need for redemption. The fulness of time was when man's question was no longer "What shall I do to inherit eternal life?" but, "Wretched man that I am! Who will deliver me from this body of death?" (Rom. 7:24).

But Romans 7 is written from the standpoint of Romans 8. Man can never admit the gravity of his predicament except from a participation in salvation from that predicament. Without that partaking of salvation the law must say that some few may be saved and induce self-righteousness in those few. Ezra's despair oscillates with self-righteousness. The publican and the Pharisee combine in the one man. The Jewish and the pagan virtues have no protection against self-righteousness and so become vices. St. Augustine has put this perfectly:

> For although some suppose that virtues which have a reference only to themselves, and are desired only on their own account, are yet true and genuine virtues, the fact is that even then they are inflated with pride, and are therefore to be reckoned vices rather than virtues. For as that which gives life to the flesh (the rational soul) is not derived from flesh, but is above it, so that

which gives blessed life to man is not derived from man, but is something above him; and what I say of man is true of every celestial power and virtue whatsoever.[6]

The Law cannot finally prepare us for Christ. Only Christ can prepare us for Christ. "God sent forth his Son made [born] of a woman, made [born] under the law to redeem them that were under the Law. . . ." So reads our Epistle for the First Sunday after Christmas. Not a *few* but only *one* obeyed the law. "Then as one man's trespass led to condemnation for all men, so one man's act of righteousness leads to acquittal and life for all men" (Rom. 5:18). And this one man was the Eternal Son of God who took our nature upon him and was perfectly obedient to God even unto the death of the Cross. "Wherefore God also hath highly exalted him, and given him a name which is above every name: That at the name of Jesus every knee should bow, of things in heaven, and things in earth, and things under the earth; And that every tongue should confess that Jesus Christ is Lord, to the glory of God the Father" (Phil. 2:9–11).

THE CIRCUMCISION OF CHRIST AND CHRISTMAS

Perhaps you will ask, "But why does our thought lead us to the Palm Sunday Epistle?" It did not. Or rather it did and it did not. For Philippians 2:9ff. is also the Epistle for the Feast of the Circumcision of our Lord Jesus Christ who, as the Collect says, was, in obedience to God, "circumcised, and obedient to the law for man" bringing to us the true circumcision of the Spirit, that is our baptism, the putting off of "the flesh" in the power of the Spirit. And this Epistle

---

[6] *The City of God*, Book XIX, ch. 25.

makes explicit again how it is that Christ is the preparation for the coming of Christ and how his birth effects our re-birth. We Christians, it says, confess a confession which shall be a cosmic confession in the end, "Jesus Christ is Lord." And this confession was won from us in the Resurrection so that we know that it was the Lord of the Cosmos whom we slew, yet who died for us. And we know that he came from where he is at God's behest and God sent him because God loved us. Our only response can be to give ourselves to him who gave himself to and for us. The only-begotten Son of God from God, by his coming and his dying and his rising has drawn from us a response we could not give of ourselves. He has drawn us into his only-begotten Sonship so that we are sons. "And because ye are sons, God hath sent forth the Spirit of his Son into your hearts, crying, Abba, Father. Wherefore thou art no more a servant [slave to the demonic powers], but a son; and if a son, then an heir of God through Christ." That was the rest of the Epistle for the First Sunday after Christmas.

EPIPHANY

This "ye" who are sons, receivers of the Spirit of the only Son, and therefore heirs of God through Christ are Gentiles as well as Jews. The Epiphany Epistle from Ephesians, therefore, grounds the ministry of St. Paul and the Church to the Gentiles in the mystery (secret) of Christ made known by the Spirit, and this was presaged by the finding out of the infant Christ by the Magi who were led to him by God that they might give him their symbolic gifts.

The propers for the Epiphany Season are remarkably correlated with the Season and with each other. This is partially due to the fact that the first four Sundays' Epistles are a well-chosen sequence from the Epistle to the Romans. In Romans 12:1–13:7 St. Paul is giving exhortation to the Church in Rome to act out what it is, the Body of Christ. On the Fifth Sunday after Epiphany, Colossians 3:12ff. rounds off the exhortation perfectly, as we shall see. The Manifestation of Christ by and through the Church might well be the title of the first five Epiphany Sundays' Epistles. The Sixth Sunday after Epiphany, which incidentally will occur only about five times in the next fifty-eight years, is also an Advent theme, designed to be used at the end of Trinity Season. The theme is the Final Manifestation of Christ when he comes in majesty and glory to destroy his enemies, judge the quick and the dead and rule perfectly and everlastingly.

The Gospels are not so obviously correlated. Two, Jesus' Baptism from St. Mark and the Miracle at Cana from St. John, have been Epiphany Gospels from the earliest days, perhaps from the origin of the season itself. The Sixth Sunday Gospel is, of course, eschatological. All the others save one portray Christ being manifest. That one is the parable of the wheat and the tares from St. Matthew's Gospel which says that the final manifestation of Christ will purge the Church of tares sowed there by the enemy.

EPIPHANY AND OUR EUCHARISTIC OBEDIENCE

Anglicans immediately think of the Eucharist when they hear Romans 12:1ff. read, even when it is not read as a proper of the celebration of the Eucharist. For it suggests, and is the source of, the words of the Church's self-oblation in the Anglican Eucharist to which it is unique. "And here we offer and present unto thee, O Lord, our selves, our souls and bodies, to be a reasonable, holy, and living sacrifice unto thee."

The Pauline Epiphany Exhortation sequence begins, "I beseech you therefore, brethren, by the mercies of God, that ye present your bodies a living sacrifice, holy, acceptable unto God, which is your reasonable service (*logiken latreian humon*). And be ye transformed by the renewing of your mind (*noos*). . . . " For St. Paul, as for Christian theology, man is psycho-somatic; he is a soulish body. This he has in common with all living beings. As Aristotle said, soul is the form which makes a thing live. Man does not differ from the cabbage or the cow in having a soul. He differs from vegetables and animals by having a *rational* soul, a different kind of soul from an animal (a-rational) soul. St. Paul's contrast, therefore, is between animal, holy and dead sacrifices and human, holy and living sacrifices. To offer our bodies to God as a living, holy sacrifice is our human (rational, reasonable) service. This means, of course, that it is a rational (human, voluntary) act not an a-rational (animal, involuntary) act. So that our reason (mind, *nous*) must also be transformed (metamorphosed) if we are not to be conformed to this age.

Judaism immediately before the New Testament had understood clearly why it sacrificed animals. Animals were non-rational. They had no freedom and were therefore sinless. Man had freedom, had misused it and could not give himself to God, for "God is of purer eyes than to behold iniquity." The sinless, animal offering was given to God as a representative of sinful but penitent man who identified himself with his offering. This representation was satisfactory because it was sinless, but it was deeply unsatisfactory because it was sub-human and involuntary. Only Christ's sacrifice resolves this intolerable human dilemma, the need to give oneself to God and our unworthiness as a gift. Jesus' sacrifice is himself. He is perfectly obedient to God in his vocation of Messiah throughout his whole life. His gift of himself on the Cross to God for man is but the depth moment of his eternal giving of himself to God for man. And his is a whole human nature with a rational soul and body, as the Council of Chalcedon has said. Included in the Incarnate Son's obedience to the Father, therefore, is the perfect human (rational) obedience to God. He alone is man's representative perfect sacrifice. But he is not only the sacrificial offering but he is also the offerer, the Priest. He gives himself. He is High Priest and Sacrifice. His self-sacrifice, consummated in the Crucifixion and Ascension, at one and the same time fulfils and abrogates animal sacrifice. "Christ, our Pascha (Passover lamb) is sacrificed for us, therefore let us keep the festival." By our faith union with Christ, as members of the one body of Christians which is his Body, the Church, we participate in his perfect offering which has replaced animal sacrifice.

The Body of Christ by its eucharistic worship is being conformed to Christ in obedience to God. We are, in unity with Christ's perfect sacrifice, "a reasonable (human), holy and living sacrifice" not "an animal, holy and dead sacri-

fice." In Christ we are acceptable to God. In his perfect
Priesthood, we are a "holy priesthood." In his perfect sacrifice, we are a human sacrifice. The Epistles of the five
Epiphany Sundays give us St. Paul working out the concrete meaning of being sacrificed to God in Christ. This
sequence from Romans with a Colossian closing is a chapter
in Christian Ethics and properly ends on a eucharistic note.
"And whatsoever ye do in word or deed, do all in the name
of the Lord Jesus, giving thanks to God and the Father by
him." "The Christian Ethic is a thank-you ethic," a sentence which I owe to a friend, the Reverend Karl Lutge.

CHRISTMAS-EPIPHANY IS THE GOSPEL

The Epiphany Gospels complete our thought. It is likely
that the Gospel first associated with Epiphany was one
which narrated the Baptism of Jesus. Epiphany was the
feast of the Manifestation of Christ to the world and the
birth of Christ and his Baptism were celebrated together.
When the Feast of the Nativity was separated out, justification of January sixth as the feast of the Manifestation of
Christ became necessary. The following quotation is from
McArthur: "On 6th January 387, the Epiphany following
the first celebration of Christmas in Antioch, Chrysostom
delivered a sermon which provides us with further informa-
tion. It is to be noted that on this occasion he uses the term
'Epiphany,' not 'Theophany,' but this does not seem to have
any particular significance. The festival is the commemoration of our Lord's Baptism. But the preacher has to explain
why the title 'Epiphany' should be applied to this festival
and not to the Birthday. . . . The answer of Chrysostom is
that in the Incarnation the Revelation was, as it were, hid-

den to the world, and that only with the Baptism was Jesus Christ manifested. . . . 'Why then is this day called Epiphany? Because it was not when He was born that He became manifest to all, but when He was baptized; for up to this day He was unknown to the majority.' " [7] St. Mark's narrative of the Baptism of Jesus is a good manifestation story although, as we have said, in St. Mark it is a manifestation of the Son of God to the post-Whitsunday Church through the ages, still hidden, according to St. Mark, from Jesus' contemporaries. In it we hear God's designation of Jesus, "Thou art my beloved Son," we see the heavens opened so that nothing intervenes between the Father and the Son, and we see the Spirit descending upon Jesus. God makes Jesus manifest to us as his Son.

St. Chrysostom, in the same sermon, gives us also the second great theme of the Baptism. Jesus, he says, "sanctified the nature of the waters." This sanctification of the baptismal waters is a New Testament theme. He who knew no sin took upon himself the sin of the world. By the identification of himself with us in our sinful situation he is baptized for the remission of sin. He is baptized for us. Given the unbreakable unity of his two natures and his unity with us in our sin, the Cross was inevitable. This is why Jesus can speak to James and John of his coming crucifixion as a baptism and unite that baptism with the cup of which he speaks in Gethsemane. When the sons of Zebedee ask for the highest places in Christ's glory, he replies:

> You do not know what you are asking. Are you able to drink the cup that I drink, or to be baptized with the baptism with which I am baptized? (Mk. 10:38)

[7] McArthur, *op. cit.*, p. 50.

As St. Paul wrote:

For our sake he [God] made him [Christ] to be sin
who knew no sin, so that in him we might become the
righteousness of God. (II Cor. 5:21)

Christ sanctified our baptismal waters and eucharistic cup
by being baptized and drinking for us.

The other Gospel associated with Epiphany from the
beginning is the miracle of the Wedding of Cana. It is
even possible, as McArthur has suggested: "that by the end
of the first century the Epiphany, the transformation of a
pagan celebration into a Christian festival, was in existence
at Ephesus, the capital of the province of Asia, the region
which at that period constituted the most vigorous area of
the Church's expansion. It was against the liturgical background of this festival that John 1:1–2:11 was written." [8]

Whatever may be the historical facts here, the theological
truth is clear. The manifestation of Christ in Cana is the
manifestation of the Logos made flesh, the only begotten
Son who took upon himself our humanity. He by his earthly
career has inaugurated the new and final age which both
fulfils and replaces the waters of purification and the wine
of joyous life offered man by Judaism and Paganism. The
Christmas and Epiphany seasons, therefore, present the
whole Gospel in correlation with and transformation of
man's understanding of his deepest need, union with God.
Preaching during these seasons seeks only this relevant
manifestation of Christ. Christmas-Epiphany unveils, and
answers with Christ, the deepest need and the true yearning
of men for God.

[8] McArthur, *op. cit.*, p. 69.

CHAPTER THREE

Preaching in Pre-Lent

BY THEODORE O. WEDEL

1

Septuagesima, Sexagesima, Quinquagesima. No Sundays in
the Church Year have names more musically appealing than
these many-syllabled refrains. To be able to roll them off the
tongue and to know what they stand for must give to the
layman a sense of accomplishment and of having been
initiated into the Church's higher learning. The uninitiate,
having consulted for their meaning a dictionary or liturgical
commentary, knows that they are datings back through the
calendar from Easter, even though the arithmetic is in-
accurate and is symbolic only. The season of Epiphany is
ended. On occasion, when Easter comes early, only one or
two Sundays fall within that season's embrace. Lent looms
ahead. A too-sudden plunge from the mood of rejoicing
during the nativity festivals to the austerities of the peni-
tential season is bridged by the Pre-Lenten weeks. There
is, accordingly, a practical value in what has been called a
"Penumbra of Lent." This brief season, "possessing traditionally the reduced solemnities of omitted *Gloria in Ex-*

celsis, Te Deum, and *Alleluia,* acts as an interlude modulating from a major to a minor key."

Has this interlude a theme of its own definite enough to give guidance for a series of sermons? If we glance through the traditional Collects, Epistles, and Gospels, we may well be puzzled at first. A unifying theme is not altogether obvious. The three Epistles, to be sure, are all taken from the Letters of St. Paul, and "present in turn the figure of the Christian soldier, the Christian's undefeated conflict with overwhelming adversity, and the final triumph of Christian charity." What these can suggest for sermon themes I shall discuss in a moment after the Matins and Evensong lessons recommended by our present lectionary have been included in our survey. A word first, however, on the Gospels for the three Sundays. These take a direction of their own. The lections consist of the parables of the Laborers in the Vineyard and of the Sower, and the account of a healing miracle of our Lord on his way to Jerusalem and the Cross. The last of these three, the one for Quinquagesima Sunday, can constitute an obvious bridge from Pre-Lent to Lent itself, since it offers a glimpse ahead to the action's climax. The choice for this season of the two preceding parables remains, however, slightly puzzling, until our liturgical scholars come to our aid and inform us that these Pre-Lenten Sundays were once New Year Sundays according to the older calendar traditional down to the middle of the eighteenth century, in which the New Year began on March twenty-fifth, a day in spring, in place of our later calendar's choice of the first day of January. Scripture passages dealing with preparation of vineyards in Mediterranean lands and the sowing of seed would have appeared appropriate. Indeed, spring being still a yearly wonder in our calendar also, even though not harboring a New Year's festival, these parables can receive a time setting even today.

The fashioners of our present lectionary suggest, accordingly, that the "liturgical Scriptures of this Season comprise intimations of a two-fold spiritual call: to arms and to labor"; and they have retained this clue to the Season's meaning in the choice of the lessons for Morning and Evening Prayer. A glance through these lections, ranging from Deuteronomy and Leviticus (a book of the Old Testament rarely read in public worship) and Joshua to the Letters to Timothy, will give evidence of the care with which the Bible has been surveyed for passages echoing the call to the Christian to "endure hardness" as a Christian soldier, to sow the seed of the Kingdom, to undergo martyrdom for the faith if necessary, and to obey the commandment of love of the Sermon on the Mount, to cite typical examples. In other words, the Season's thematic meaning has been interpreted, to quote our present liturgical guides once more, as affording "a further integration of the moral applications of the Incarnation which have been found in Epiphany-tide," as throwing "an increased emphasis on religion as being dynamic, not escapist," and as presenting "salvation as wrought in us, rather than for us." [1]

As those familiar with the rationale of our present American version of the Book of Common Prayer know, our currently authorized lectionary in the Episcopal Church

[1] All the quotations in the above paragraphs are from Bayard F. Jones, *The American Lectionary* (New York: Morehouse-Gorham, 1944), pp. 62–63.

employs as a guide to the choice of lessons for our Sunday prayer offices conformity with the themes suggested by the Propers for the Eucharist of that day and week. Without attempting a critical evaluation of this principle of choice, it is at least interesting, on occasion, to compare the outcome with other lectionaries in the Anglican family of churches. For the Pre-Lenten season this comparison yields a particularly valuable result. The lectionary of the Church of England, like that of the Episcopal Church of Scotland, preserves a lectionary tradition for the Pre-Lenten season going back to the medieval Church and retained and even highlighted to this day in the Roman Breviary. Septuagesima, even if a shifting date on the calendar, once paralleled, as already noted, the secular calendar's New Year's Day. Whether because of this correspondence, or because of theological appropriateness, the Pre-Lenten and Lenten seasons were dedicated to the Book of Genesis. A Roman Catholic comment ("Septuagesima," *Catholic Encyclopaedia*) points out, somewhat wistfully, that Pre-Lent is the one season in the Church Year when Adam is given proper attention in the public worship of the Church. In long-traditional Anglican lectionaries, at any rate, the Old Testament lections for both Morning and Evening Prayer are taken from these matchless opening pages of Holy Scripture. In thousands of churches in the Anglican Communion, the worshippers at the prayer offices will hear read, on Septuagesima Sunday, Genesis 1 and 2; on Sexagesima Sunday, Genesis 3 and 6 or 8 (the story of Noah); and on Quinquagesima Sunday, Genesis 12 and 13 (the calling of Abraham).

The pulpit in the Anglican tradition, while it rightly remains respectful of an official lectionary and is encouraged to utilize for sermon themes the eucharistic Propers or the prayer office lessons for the day, is not in a strait-jacket. Surely, the older lection tradition of beginning the Pre-Lenten season with the reading of Genesis can offer for sermon themes an alternative to those which derive from our newer lesson roster. Indeed, sermons on Adam and Eve and the Fall, as on the succeeding stories with which the Scriptural record of revelation opens, can find encouragement even in our present American lectionary as it stands in the fact that the weekday Old Testament lections for Morning Prayer for the days following Septuagesima Sunday and running on to Ash Wednesday pay tribute to the older lectionary tradition by a choice precisely of the Book of Genesis.

We have before us, then, as lectionary guides to our preaching in the Pre-Lenten season, at least two thematic suggestions—the one summarizing in effect our American lectionary's harvest of Scriptural selections as "a call to arms and labor" and, as an alternative, the mighty act of Creation and the story of Adam and the other opening scenes in the Biblical drama of redemption which culminates in the events of Cross and Resurrection and Pentecost and which the Church Year will memorialize shortly in their turn.

As we look for a space at the first of these alternatives, we meet themes which at first sight look as if they could be easily moulded into homiletic forms, yet which, on second sight, present difficulties. When I was a boy, in the days of Theodore Roosevelt's rule as President of the land, the phrase "the strenuous life" became popular. It fits into our American temper to this day. Every European observer of our social scene and of our church life notes what has come to be called our "activism." The figure of the athlete running a race, or of the soldier assaulting enemy beaches, symbolizes much of our popular view of what Christianity is all about. It is fight against evil. It is the strenuosity of moral striving, with the Golden Rule and Sermon on the Mount a kind of goal line. The Epistle for Septuagesima, with its picture of a runner in a race at a track meet, followed in the Epistle for Sexagesima with the sketch of a model Gospel athlete in the story of the literally astounding strenuous hero-life of St. Paul (thrice beaten with rods, shipwrecked, stoned), followed, in turn, by the Epistle for Quinquagesima, picturing the ideal of the Christian life as perfect charity (the goal line again)—here is a series of Scripture lessons which a typical American congregation, particularly if not yet past middle age, thinks it can readily understand. Most of the hymns which our Hymnal Commission recommends for the Pre-Lenten season undergird this call to arms and labor in the Christian life. I cite a few typical first lines: "Breast the wave, Christian"; "Fight the good fight with all thy might"; "He who would valiant be"; "Oft in danger, oft in woe, Onward, Christian, onward go"; "Awake my soul, stretch every nerve"; and, still in this mood, "Come labor on. Who dares stand idle on the harvest plain?"

The Christian life as the strenuous life; the appeal for striving to bring in the Kingdom of God on earth; reminders of the fact that at Baptism we were commissioned Christ's faithful soldiers and servants so that we should fight manfully under his banner against sin, the world, and the devil: who can deny that exhortations to activism and good works are deeply anchored in Holy Scripture, and not least in the New Testament and even the letters of St. Paul, despite the fact that the Apostle's summarizing of the Good News as justification by grace through faith seems to contradict any efficacy of a gospel of salvation by works. Whenever the counsel of St. James that "faith without works is dead" has been forgotten or neglected, Christianity has degenerated into theory-religion divorced from life, or into an escapist flight from the stern demands of the God of the Bible. The Bible can be anthologized so as to leave only a sentimental spiritualism as a final resultant. One of Rousseau's famous remarks about his mistress, Mme. de Warens, illustrates what can happen when morality is divorced from religion as mere feeling. Rousseau said of his mistress that "her actions were reprehensible, but her heart was pure." More than one version of the Christian faith which equates it with a vague mysticism or escapist spirituality desperately needs the correction of a call to effort and ethical earnestness. We dare not divorce religion and morals.

Yet a little thought and a little viewing of this call to a Christianity of good works in the perspective of the Bible as a whole can warn us that a preaching of it can run into difficulties. Divorce it from the doctrines clustering about the concepts of original sin and of grace, of judgment and the atoning Cross, and it can play into the hands of the humanist and the secular idealist. A generation ago, during the still-not-disillusioned era of an optimistic doctrine of man, a view of Christianity as nothing more than ethical idealism and an invitation to men to exert their powers to achieve moral perfection was equated with the essence of the Gospel. That era is fortunately on its way out, though thousands among our lay people still live within its embrace. The Pelagian heresy once called upon all the efforts of St. Augustine to reveal its errors. Augustinianism has had to receive revival in the schools in our day, and we can be grateful for the revolution. Richard Niebuhr's satiric description of our modern Pelagianism can still stir us awake whenever we are tempted to give in to the popular view of Christianity as man on the march under the banner of his own powers: "A God without wrath brought men without sin into a kingdom without judgment through the ministrations of a Christ without a cross." [2] "Come labor on." But labor for what? Even the call to be a soldier assumes that you have a recruit able to bear arms. It is obvious that such a call, if ethical perfectionism is the proposed goal, can be utter bad news leading to despair for the alcoholic on skid row or for any of the victims of demonic powers of evil. Preach it to publicans and sinners yet unrescued by a Gospel of grace, and they may leave your church with a curse against God on their lips. We would be fortunate if we could hold their attention until we sing our strangely different Lenten hymns.

[2] H. Richard Niebuhr, *The Kingdom of God in America* (Chicago: Willett, Clark & Co., 1937), p. 193.

Weary of earth, and laden with my sins,
I look at heav'n and long to enter in,
But there no evil thing may find a home:
And yet I hear a voice that bids me, "Come."

or

Art thou weary, art thou laden,
Art thou sore distrest?
"Come to me," saith One,
"And coming, Be at rest."

I trust that we are not overwhelmed with too great a surprise to find that the supposedly stern theme of Lent, with its call to repentance, can, for many a listener, actually come as welcome good news by way of contrast with the burden of the Pre-Lenten call to the strenuous life. Set over against each other the "Be at rest" of the Lenten hymn just quoted and "Fight the good fight" of the hymn which we may sing on Septuagesima Sunday, and we plainly confront a paradox.

Can the paradox be solved? Of course it can if we conquer the temptation to preach the Pre-Lenten themes divorced from their context in the full round of Christian faith and as mere Pelagian flattery of the powers of the natural man. We confront then in Holy Scripture, and in the faith which we are commanded to proclaim, the majestic paradox of Law and Grace.

You will, I trust, not expect a comprehensive solution of this central paradox of the Bible in the brief space here allotted to me. The whole of the Biblical revelation, from Creation to the Vision of a new heaven and earth, wrestles with it. I shall venture only a few suggestions which may stimulate further thought as we meditate on our Pre-Lenten sermon themes.

We may well remind ourselves at the outset that moral exhortations and imperatives meet us in the Bible in a context and with a meaning very different from the context and meaning which the secular philosophers can find for them. The moral demands of Biblical faith are, in the first place, not ideals. The demands voiced in the Bible are commandments of a living and even "terrible" God (Deut. 7:21, 10:17, for example). How much harm has been done to the understanding of Christianity on the part of multitudes in our time by interpreting it as mere moral idealism we shall probably never know. Ideals can be the product of man's own imagination, and when thus created by ourselves or even when voiced by a master of human wisdom speaking to us out of the past, there is nothing "terrible" about them. Failure to achieve conduct corresponding to the ideal may produce modest in place of immodest boasting, but it need not give us a sense of sin at all. An ideal which we could achieve would cease to be an ideal. Its value consists precisely in being set in a moral stratosphere, and we judge a neighbor frequently not so much by his conduct as by the ideals he professes. We certainly are tempted to judge ourselves by this easy test. When we hear a layman who is indifferent to Church attendance offering the excuse that he "lives by" the Golden Rule and the Sermon on the Mount and considers this enough to label himself a good Christian, he surely does not mean that he is an exemplar of moral perfection under these idealistic demands. He means simply that here is a standard of conduct which he admires and which he, in his moments of aspiration, is willing to honor as an ethical goal line. The poet Browning should, perhaps, not be personally blamed for the use made of one of his most quoted couplets, but it has had dangerous results. I refer to the familiar lines:

> Oh, but a man's reach should exceed his grasp,
> Or what's a heaven for.

Some at least of our parishioners, still living by the easy Christianity of moral idealism, will have little difficulty in singing our stirring Pre-Lenten hymns:

> He who would valiant be
> 'Gainst all disaster,
> Let him in constancy
> Follow the Master.

But will they realize what this really means? To interpret this hymn, and others like it, under the full demand of the Gospel is no light task.

I am not, may I hasten to say, trying to expurgate our hymnal or our Pre-Lenten lectionary. I merely wish to call attention to the vocation we encounter in dealing wisely with the deeply anchored Pelagian heresy of our time. Some of our people who, on Septuagesima Sunday, will enjoy singing Bunyan's noble hymn, will interpret it as little more than an appeal directed to their own moral idealism—in final view, to themselves as their own saviors. The self-idolatry that lies in wait for those who confess Christianity as nothing more than ethical striving for a self-defined goal, however high and lofty, is tragically hidden from their sight.

We return, then, to our task of preaching the Law as we meet it in the Bible, in contrast to the "law" when it is reduced to the form of ideals. The Law as we meet it in the Bible, as already indicated, confronts us in the form of commandments. These are voiced in the thunderings of the sacred mountain of the Old Testament and in the words, equally awesome if understood as once again divine demands, spoken from the sermon-mountain of the Gospel record. In these contexts the demands directed to the moral life of man are no longer invitations to an easy dialogue with the ideals of our better selves or the good advice of a professor of ethics, but with the Creator of heaven and earth, the Judge of all men. We are in the midst of an encounter with One who has our eternal destiny in his hands. This Law, unlike an impersonal ideal, comes with power. He who voices these demands wields sanctions for their performance. These sanctions are presented to us inexorably throughout the Bible, in the Revelation of St. John the Divine as well as in Exodus and Deuteronomy. "It shall come to pass, if thou shalt hearken diligently unto the voice of the Lord thy God . . . Blessed shalt thou be in the city, and blessed shalt thou be in the field. . . . But it shall come to pass, if thou wilt not hearken unto the voice of the Lord thy God . . . Cursed shalt thou be in the city, and cursed shalt thou be in the field" (Deut. 28:1, 3, 15–16). Thus the voice of the divine Lawgiver addresses us in the Old Testament. "I am Alpha and Omega, the first and the last—and have the keys of hell and of death" (Rev. 1:8, 18). Thus, the Christ of the New Testament meets us as final Judge in the Bible's closing vision.

Have we the courage to preach the Pre-Lenten themes of moral warfare and ethical striving in this context of the Law as we meet it in Holy Scripture? Can we assume that its eschatological framework is sufficiently implanted in the minds of our hearers so that they will take the demands of the Law seriously enough, with fear of eternal doom as a sanction, and that they will know where to turn if they suffer shipwreck on the way of attempted performance? "So run that ye may obtain," reads our Septuagesima Epistle. If we should interpret literally the preceding phrase which, in introducing this picture of a footrace, alludes to the fact that all participants run, but only "one receiveth the prize," and if they are not among the prize-winners, have we possibly preached a message which leaves their last state worse than their first?

To preach Christianity as a religion of moral effort looks easy at first. Our people will welcome it so long as it pictures the Christian life as within their powers of performance. But performance is precisely what the Law in the Bible will show us to be an illusion—particularly if we let it confront us in its climactic form in the Sermon on the Mount and in the example of the Incarnate Son of God. To forgive seventy times seven? To see the demands of Deuteronomy reinterpreted so that they ask for purity of heart as well as of action, for absence of lust and envy as well as avoidance of outward harm to our neighbor? If we look again at our Pre-Lenten hymns, since the layman's theology is so largely moulded by the songs he sings, we can probably confess that it is thrilling to join in "Fight the good fight with all thy might," or in "Awake, my soul, stretch every nerve." But what is the use of all this effort if it never succeeds? Something is still wrong with the context of the "call to arms and to labor" if it is pictured as an isolated demand for perfectionist moral obedience to the Law. This, to the publicans and sinners of the world, is still bad news.

For a full solution of the paradox of Law and Grace, we must, accordingly, as everyone familiar with the whole drama of the Bible can tell us, look again. The Law's demands must be taken with absolute seriousness. Otherwise we are worshipping an idol. The God of the Bible is a holy God. But the function of the Law is not ended by revealing to us the holiness of God or the inexorability of his demands or the sanctions of heaven and hell which place them in an eschatological framework. The Law is, in St. Paul's word, the "schoolmaster" or pedagogue to bring us to Christ. Failure to obey it is, as it were (though this is dangerous to say), expected by the Lawgiver. It summons us to obedience always. But its deeper summons is to repentance, a repentance which, we should note, would be a sham if it had not been preceded by trial obedience and then by the inevitable failure. The Law convicts us of sin. It kills our pride. In place of trying to escape its death-dealing powers, we are letting it fulfil its function if we permit it to evoke the cry, "Who then can be saved?" or the publican's prayer: "God be merciful to me, a sinner." The Law prepares us for the acceptance of Grace. Only against the background of acknowledged failure to keep the Law will the call to penitence be good news. The Pre-Lenten call to arms and labor looked as if it were easily heard and obeyed.

The Lenten call to the austerities of penance looked hard. Paradox leads into paradox. The order of easy and hard exhortations of the seasons is virtually reversed. In comparison with the despair of failure before the fully revealed Law of God, the despair of repentance looms up as sheer joy. At last we can let go our pride, and sing: "Just as I am, without one plea, O Lamb of God, I come."

The good news of repentance, however, need not be expounded further here. It will be the theme for the Lenten season itself. We are not quite at the end of giving to the Pre-Lenten message its place in the full round of the Biblical revelation.

For, obviously, the good news of repentance is not the whole of the good news of the Gospel, either. This good news is but the first movement in the symphony of the Gospel of Grace which our Bible and our Hymnal and our Liturgy invite us to sing in gratitude to God. Cross and Resurrection, Ascension and Pentecost will be the movements of this symphony of memorial awaiting us at the close of Lent. And it is only at the end of this full round of memorial that the Law as exhortation to performance can fully come into its own. For now it can receive the motivation of gratitude. The Law remains the Law. But failure to fulfil it has not had to end in despair. Grace has intervened. "Guilt," so reads a memorable sentence in the *Letters* of St. Ambrose, "was indeed increased by the Law, but pride, the author of this guilt, was overthrown by it." Or, to quote from St. Augustine: "The guilt of the Law made the sickness of the proud; the sickness of the proud became the confession of the humble; the sick now confess that they are sick; let the physician come." [3] And, to complete the cycle, after the resurrection of forgiveness has ushered the repentant sinner into the new life of Grace, we meet the Law once more. Obedience to its demands is now, however, motivated by grateful penitence. It is now fruit of the Holy Spirit.

I shall not burden your attention with further review of what is familiar to us as we cast memory back to the picture in the New Testament of the new life in Christ. St. Paul summarizes it unforgettably in his Epistle to the Ephesians. We are saved by grace through faith unto good works (Ephes. 2:8-10). The Pilgrimage from finding ourselves guilty under the Law through death with Christ in repentance and rising again with him in the acceptance of forgiveness ends with the renewal in gratitude of the baptismal vow to become Christ's soldier and servant.

As we confront the task of preaching the Pre-Lenten theme of "a call to arms and labor," the thought may occur to us that it should come rightly at the end of the Church Year's memorial of the drama of redemption. Do not the fruits of the Spirit await the empowering of Pentecost? The difficulties in presenting the life of the Christian soldier without leading our hearers into the idolatry of moralism and self-salvation have surely been sufficiently stressed earlier. This danger is real. Yet, if the call to the strenuous life of the Christian, nurtured by our stirring martial hymns,

[3] St. Ambrose, *Letters*, lxxiii, 9. St. Augustine, *Homilies on St. John*, iii, 21. Both of these citations I owe to Alec Vidler's *Christ's Strange Work* (London: Longmans Green, 1944), p. 43—an excellent treatment of the place of Law in Christian faith.

can be presented in the full context of the covenant theology of the Bible, the Pre-Lenten season can, indeed, be a bridge between the festive memorials of the Nativity and of Epiphany and the austerities of Lent. "Fight the good fight with all thy might," so we sing our Septuagesima recruiting song. The fight, seen in the perspective of the whole Gospel, may have to be, first of all, an attack upon our own pride. The race which we are to run may have as its first goal line the home to which a prodigal son returns to find forgiveness in a Father's arms. Gratitude for the banquet which meets us in the Father's household may then move us to enlist in his army and to fight his war against his enemies. The Christian soldier is recruited from among those who have first been conquered and been taken prisoner by the love of God in Christ and have then been set free again under the "perfect law of liberty" of the Gospel (James 1:25). They are the dead and the resurrected, those who have died with Christ and have risen with him in the deep waters of baptism. Other recruitment the army of the Lord does not know.

The Epistle to the Ephesians places the Pre-Lenten call to arms in the right context. "You hath he quickened, who were dead in trespasses and sins; wherein in time past ye walked. . . . By grace are ye saved through faith; and that not of yourselves: it is the gift of God" (Ephes. 2:1, 8). Only after being empowered with this gift does the Apostle ask us to accept the vocation of the Christian soldier. "Take unto you the whole armor of God . . . having your loins girt about with truth . . . And your feet shod with the preparation of the gospel" (Ephes. 6:13–15). Any other weapons or armor, such as we might fashion ourselves with ever-so-high ambitions to win moral victories over the enemy, will fail in combat. "For we wrestle not against flesh and blood, but against principalities, against powers, against the rulers of the darkness of this world, against spiritual wickedness in high places" (Ephes. 6:12).

II

Attention has already been called to the fact that a lectionary tradition older than the one now official in our American Book of Common Prayer constitutes an alternative cluster of themes for pulpit use during the Pre-Lenten season—namely, the themes which derive from the opening chapters of Genesis. Whether these lections, once traditional for the three Sundays preceding Ash Wednesday, can be substituted in our prayer offices when used in public worship in place of our officially appointed Scripture passages, I must leave to individual rubrical conscience. In the pulpit, however, their use will violate no legal prohibitions. The recurring round of the Church Year surely permits our exposition of Holy Scripture in the pulpit both to be loyal to officially sponsored Bible lections and to be venturesome by way of responsible departures—particularly if the choice of an alternative remains within the compass of catholic tradition. The opening scenes in the drama or epic of revelation recorded in the Book of Genesis, as I indicated earlier, have this validation even within the Anglican Communion. I proceed, accordingly, to discuss some of the enticing possibilities of this alternative cluster of themes for Pre-Lenten preaching.

Indeed, I shall go further. I shall urge that we owe to the Book of Genesis our full attention in the pulpit and that the Pre-Lenten season offers a peculiarly advantageous setting for homiletic presentation of its profound significance for Christian faith. Our official lectionary cannot be accused of wholly neglecting these matchless chapters of the Bible. The first chapter of Genesis is our lectionary's second choice for an Old Testament lesson on Trinity Sunday. The third chapter is similarly offered as second choice on the First Sunday after Trinity, with other selected passages from among the Genesis narratives listed as third choices for other Sundays in the Trinity season. We can welcome them there and yet see value in bringing them into prominence precisely in the interlude between Epiphany and Lent. The Church Year, from Advent through Pentecost, memorializes the mighty acts of God in the New Testament revelation, with Good Friday and Easter climactic in the story. But knowledge of the Old Testament is largely assumed. The second Adam has crowded the first Adam off the stage—and rightly so in final view, of course. Yet a neglect in Christian teaching of the meaning for the new covenant of the older of the two testaments can have unhappy results. An Old Testament lection has even dropped out of the Word Service of the Eucharist. We are inclined to forget that the early Church knew no canonical Scriptures except the Old Testament. Even the sermons recorded in the Acts of the Apostles are largely expositions of its prophetic wonders. The Gospel of Cross and Resurrection cannot be understood except in the perspective of the whole "plot" of the Bible. We need a knowledge of the *dramatis personae* in the long historic dialogue between God and man. We need to know ourselves as sons of Adam as well as sons of God which we may become through the atoning act of Christ. As background for the journey to the Cross memorialized in Lent and Passiontide, the story of how it all began, in man's rebellion against his Creator, offers incomparable sermon themes.

It is clearly noteworthy that one of the signs of the "return to orthodoxy" in the theological schools of our day is precisely the emergence into prominence once more of the doctrines of Creation and the Fall. We may even see the emergence shortly in our dictionaries of a new word—*Ktisiology*. Borrowed from the Greek word for creation, it is already current in advanced theological discourse, and its increased use is symbolic of the rediscovered importance of the doctrine which it defines.

The era of so-called Liberalism tried its best to belittle the realism of man's expulsion from the garden of Eden. In that era it was fashionable to ignore the doctrine of original sin as if it were an affront to the essential goodness of human nature. A doctrine of Creation, yes, of course. Even modern science has to assume some kind of myth of a beginning of the world in time. But please, not a doctrine of the Fall! This humanistic era, however, found out to its cost that the whole "plot" of the Biblical story becomes meaningless without the event of the Fall which sets the scene. There can be no redemption if there is nothing to redeem. Today, fortunately, the realism of the Bible has come into its own again, and in nothing more significantly than the appreciation of the crucial importance of the Book of

Genesis. Karl Barth devotes a whole volume of his massive *Dogmatik* (III, 1) to virtually the first three chapters. Emil Brunner similarly emphasizes these chapters in one of the volumes of his systematic theology—a volume entitled *Creation and Redemption*. Few topics in the realm of theological investigation are more fiercely debated today than the doctrine of Man, particularly the phrase in the first chapter of Genesis describing man as created in God's image.[4]

An acquaintance with the theological discourse carried on by the learned doctors in the schools is invaluable for the preacher (I would even call it indispensable), but we cannot transfer such debate into the pulpit. There our vocation is to let the Holy Scriptures speak directly through us to our people, permitting Biblical and theological scholarship to have their say in our homiletic workshops behind the scenes. The question then confronts us: What, under the guidance of the Spirit, do these opening chapters of the Bible say to the listening people of God in our day and generation? I make bold to present for your consideration some tentative answers to this question.

Is the doctrine of Creation of more than academic interest to the man in the street today? Has it, to employ the fashionable jargon of our time, any existential meaning? On superficial view, it would seem that this is one doctrine which we could pass over lightly in presenting the Christian faith. The number of atheists in our flocks is not large.

[4] Good summaries of the debate swirling about this crucial Biblical symbol are: David Cairns, *The Image of God* (London: Student Christian Movement Press, 1953); and John Baillie, *Our Knowledge of God* (New York: Charles Scribner's Sons, 1939).

Nor will there be many who come to us with a soul hungering for the cosmological proof for the existence of God. Of course he exists, or some mysterious X to which the world and we in it owe our existence and to which we might as well apply the traditional name. The gospel of Friedrich Nietszche that God is dead, or the philosophy of the contemporary existentialists of Europe, has not penetrated far into the life of suburbia in America. Sometimes one could wish that it had, since then the revelation in the Bible of a Creator and Maker of heaven and earth might be seen again as crucial for a saving faith.

Yet, if we look beneath the surface of even the outwardly god-believing life of men and women in contemporary suburbia, we might discover that it is precisely their attitude toward the doctrine of Creation which is as much the clue to their soul's state as it is to the soul's state of those in the covenant of Grace or those wandering in the desert of loneliness and estrangement. The existential question which this doctrine of Creation asks every man, when it ceases to be a mere propositional truth of academic theology and turns into personal encounter-theology, can be little short of devastating to our religious calm. "Know ye that the Lord he is God; it is he that hath made us, and not we ourselves" (Psalm 100:3). Quite so. But do you like the product? Do you accept yourself joyously as, without your choosing, you find yourself hurled into existence? You did not will to be born. You may not, strange as this may seem, be able to will going out of existence, despite the apparent possibility of bodily suicide. Furthermore, the conditions of our existence, the *where* of our place of birth, the economic

state of our parents, our endowment of body and mind—
none of these were in the power of our choosing. If they
fall short of our heart's desire, and are frequently on the
edge of permanent handicap, is it easy to forgive the Creator? Is not the life of most of us, as we find it revealed to
us in moments of painful insight, one long struggle with
envy and jealousy and rebellion against our fate? Shakespeare voices a confession which I at least could make my
own:

> Wishing me like to one more rich in hope,
> Featured like him, like him with friends possess'd,
> Desiring this man's art and that man's scope,
> With what I most enjoy contented least.[5]

I recently ventured to preach a sermon on the verse of
the hundredth Psalm quoted in the previous paragraph—
"It is he that hath made us and not we ourselves"—and
gave to the sermon a title in the form of a question: "Why
do I have to be 'me'?" The men and women of suburbia to
whom many of us are directing our preaching are haunted
by that pitiful cry. D. Riesman's *The Lonely Crowd* pictures the life of our times with painful accuracy. Kierkegaard's *Sickness Unto Death* penetrates its façade on an
even deeper level. The despair of not willing to be oneself,
the frantic search for a mask behind which to hide, or one
which can deceptively set on its wearer a higher value in
the market—these are signs of the deep-seated rebellion
against the Creator which constitutes the background for
the preaching of the Gospel in our time.

Add to this the fateful gift or burden of freedom which

[5] From Sonnet 29.

makes man himself responsible for what he, as creator in his turn, does with his given endowments, and which plunges him into the bottomless bog of guilt—and the Creator has on his hands creatures who, in the depths of their being, hurl indictments against him. Sartre, our contemporary French philosopher, has coined the phrase, "Man is condemned to be free." Our freedom and sense of responsibility is the climactic insult which the Creator, if there be a God, has perpetrated on his helpless creatures. "Am I a sea, or a whale, that thou settest a watch over me? Why hast thou set me as a mark against thee, so that I am a burden to myself? Let me alone," cries Job (Job 7:12, 16, 20). The Bible is a very existentialist book. Atheists might well quote it more frequently.

Oh, I know that we are rarely as honest as the atheist philosopher or Job. We do not like to reveal even to ourselves our envy of our neighbors or our hatred of our Creator. Both neighbor and God might retaliate. Even religion can become mere propitiation and the attempt to ward off further unjust manifestations of the power of him who hath made us and not we ourselves. Our rebellion against the Creator can manifest itself in the very heart of the religious life itself. The first picture of the relationship between man and his human brother that we meet in the Bible is the story of a murder before an altar. Cain's hatred is directed more against God than against Abel. Was it not God's doing that Abel's offering found an acceptance denied to that of Cain? Murder in the form of jealousy and cruel rivalry for preferred acceptance of our offerings—be it even in the form of heroic service on a mission field—

is not unknown in the household of God today. We are all Cain as well as Abel. Each one of us, surely, recognizes himself, on occasions at least, as the man of one talent in the Gospel parable who nurses an inferiority complex and who hurls an indictment against his Lord. "Lord, I knew thee that thou art an hard man, reaping where thou hast not sown, and gathering where thou hast not strawed" (Matt. 25:24).

The allusion to the fateful gift of freedom as part of our human endowment as we emerge on the scene of the created order ushers us into the presence of the climactic verse of the Creation chapter of the Bible. "And God said, let us make man in our own image." Man, the image of God! This little jewel-phrase contains in miniature, as it were, the clue to the whole breath-taking drama of the Bible. I shall not attempt here a review of the theological debate, alluded to earlier, which in our era of theological revival swirls about this little formula. The debate is itself proof of the importance of this key to the doctrine of man in the Bible. Suffice it to say that our Biblical theologians are today largely at one in seeing man's uniqueness in creation as consisting, not primarily in his rational endowment, but in man's will, in his power of decision, and his transcendence over himself as a responsible being. Man is free to say Yes or No even to his Creator. Man, if we venture a glance forward from the doctrine of Creation to the doctrine of the Last Things, is the unique being in the universe who can go to Hell.

The creation of man has been called "God's great adventure." The closing verses of the third chapter of Genesis, often neglected, I fear, because of the overshadowing impact upon the reader of the story of the Fall which precedes them, are filled with meaning. God is pictured there as if in consultation with himself or his advisers and fearful of his own act in creating a rival to himself. "Behold, the man is become as one of us, to know good and evil." Man remains a potential rival to his Creator throughout the story of the Bible. That story will be a love story, God humbling himself to be the wooer of a hoped-for bride. Man, however, remains free to resist the divine wooing. He can, at the end, like Judas as pictured in the Acts of the Apostles (1:25), retain his pride of rebellion and "go to his own place."

Modern technological man, for some generations at least, found it easy to believe in his godlike endowments. Had he not become "master of things," creator of pyramids of power through the exercise of his gift of reason? He is being reminded, however, by the events of our time that his Creator has set limits to the equality of man with deity. We need merely read to the end of the chapter in Genesis in which this equality is acknowledged by God to see where boundaries are set. Man remains under the bondage of finitude. He must die. "Man," so read the concluding verses, "is become as one of us, to know good and evil: and now, lest he put forth his hand, and take also of the tree of life, and eat, and live for ever: Therefore the Lord God sent him forth from the garden of Eden. . . . So he drove out the man: and he placed at the east of the garden of Eden cherubim, and a flaming sword" (Gen. 3:22-24).

"It is dangerous," says Pascal, "to prove to man too

plainly how nearly he is on a level with the brutes without showing him his greatness; it is also dangerous to show him his greatness too clearly apart from his vileness. It is still more dangerous to leave him in ignorance of both." [6]

In our presentations of the Biblical doctrine of man to our people, both sides of the paradox of the greatness and littleness of man must, clearly, receive their due weight. For it is only the Biblical paradox which can save modern man from a two-fold illusion about himself—the illusion that he is a little godlet who, with a little more science and social manipulation can fashion a human utopia, and a second illusion, strangely contradictory of the first, that he is innocent of the evil in the world which stands in the way of such progress toward human happiness. Evil, so he assures himself, exists outside of man—in the biological lag of evolution, in the imperfection of his endocrine glands, or in the tyranny of outdated economic systems. The Biblical paradox replies to the pride of man in his own powers with the *memento mori* of the flaming sword before the garden of Eden, and to the second illusion of man's innocence with the doctrine of original sin.

I can recall a discussion hour which, along with others, I was privileged to enjoy with the late Archbishop William Temple. He was asked to define briefly the Christian doctrine of man. He replied that he could summarize all he knew of this doctrine in four words—namely, "Man is a sinner."

To unlock for our people the good as well as the bad

[6] Blaise Pascal, *Thoughts* (The York Library, London: George Bell & Sons, 1905), p. 46.

news of the Biblical doctrine of man as sinner ought to be
for us one of our joyous privileges. G. K. Chesterton once
put this paradox into a memorable sentence: "The glad
good news brought by the Gospel was the news of original
sin." [7] An exhaustive examination of this paradox, and the
long wrestlings in the history of Christian thought which
have tossed it to and fro, would lead us far. The theological
debate between supralapsarians and infralapsarians and the
daring welcome with which St. Augustine hailed the news
of the Fall by exclaiming "O felix culpa" (O happy fault),
or the profound analysis of the wonder of entrance into
Christian faith by "becoming a sinner" which fill the pages
of Kierkegaard are only a few instances of the deep things
of God which theologians have discovered in pondering
the story of Adam and Eve. I shall not take you on a
journey through these theological delights, even if I were
equipped to be your guide. Surely, in our preaching, we can
trust the Biblical story itself and discover at least some of
the mysteries which it symbolizes in our own experience.

Sin is a word shopworn in the pulpit. And if all that the
word conveys to our listeners is its legalistic and ethical
connotations, the good news which it enshrines remains
hidden from our sight. A mere moralistic use of it extracts
it from its context in the covenant religion of the Bible. It
is not surprising that the secular reformer, however high he
lets his moral idealism soar, or permits his hatred of crime
and evil free play, cannot honestly use it. One wonders
what is happening to it in atheist Russia. For, in the Biblical

[7] G. K. Chesterton, *St. Francis of Assisi* (New York: George H. Doran Co., 1924), p. 39.

context, sin implies a personal relationship. There is One who cares about our actions, who therefore judges, and who even honors the dignity of man by way of poured out wrath and by punishment. To be a sinner is sign and token of the greatness of man. Only a being created in the image of God could exercise his godlike endowment in rebellion.

It ought not to come to us as too great a surprise, accordingly, that the picturing of a godless world which our existentialist philosophers and some of our novelists and poets are presenting to us can be employed by us as a kind of inverted gospel. We can employ descriptions of the life of modern suburbia when it is an escape from repentance by way of yielding to the idolatries of worldliness similarly for the purpose of highlighting the wonders of the Gospel. The tragedy of the world outside the embrace of Biblical faith is precisely that it has no Judge! Human life becomes, as Sartre sees it, simply "absurd." If we had the power to overhear the sad music of the heart in the lives of men and women who, in Stoic pride, refuse to "become" sinners, we would be moved to pity and fear. The pharisee in our pews is in similar state. Like his prototype in the New Testament parable, he prays with his own godlike self. His loneliness, if not replaced by fellowship with God and his neighbors in repentance, can become the loneliness of hell.

To preach the good news of "becoming" a sinner is not easy. It will seem to many a listener as if we were interpreting literally St. Paul's daring words: "Shall we continue in sin that grace may abound?" Kierkegaard, conscious, of course, that he was similarly presenting a dangerous paradox, berates the easy conscience of his day of bourgeois morality: "So rather let us sin, sin out and out, seduce maidens, murder men, commit highway robbery—after all, that can be repented of, and such a criminal God can still get a hold on." [8] Yet, by way of seeing the paradox of the good news of man as a sinner, we can penetrate a little the mystery enshrined in the words of the Jesus of the Gospel story—shocking today as they once were to his contemporaries—"Verily I say unto you, That the publicans and the harlots go into the kingdom of God before you" (Matt. 21:31).

I see no heavier burden placed upon the preacher in prosperous and contented suburbia today than that of transforming the self-trusting and self-righteous into sinners, to reveal to them their estrangement from God, and to usher them by way of "becoming sinners" into the fellowship of forgiven prodigal sons. Man, in his rebellious freedom, remains forever in the outer darkness of lonely despair until, to quote Kierkegaard once more, "by the help of the torments of a contrite heart, he learns to enter by the narrow way, through the consciousness of sin, into Christianity." [9]

What the life of man might have been like had there not been a Fall, we do not know. Even the Bible places at the beginning of all history, a Lamb "slain from the foundation of the world" (Rev. 13:8). No other state than that of fallen man, created in freedom in the image of God, is known to us. But once we grasp the good news of original sin—namely, that it is proof already of a covenant relationship with a Creator God who cares, who judges and re-

[8] Søren Kierkegaard, *Concluding Unscientific Postscript* (Princeton University Press, 1941), p. 485.
[9] *Training in Christianity* (Princeton University Press, 1947), pp. 70-71.

deems—we can describe the hard road of the "sawdust trail" of repentance as the highroad to the joys of heaven. Bishop Westcott is worth listening to on the "good news" of the Fall: "No view of the human state," he says, "is so inexpressibly sad as that which leaves out the Fall. The existence of evil in its many forms, as self-will, and suffering and vice and crime, cannot be gainsaid; and if this evil belongs to the essence of man as created, then there can be no prospect of relief here or hereafter." [10] A falling presupposes a step or a rising from which to fall, as a divorce presupposes a marriage. Quite as Chesterton said: "If I wish to dissuade a man from drinking his tenth whiskey and soda, I slap him on the back and say, 'Be a man!' No one who wished to dissuade a crocodile from eating its tenth explorer would slap him on the back and say, 'Be a crocodile!' " [11]

The above are only passing reminders of the wealth of insight into our human situation contained in these matchless opening chapters of our Bible. They do not, except in a prophetic word or two, as yet contain the full Gospel. They antedate even the covenant of the Law of Sinai. Perhaps that is the reason why some of us have been tempted to pass them over lightly. They describe man's condition before grace has come with the story of redemption. But that may constitute their peculiar value for preaching in our day. The familiar symbols of religion and concepts of theology have become meaningless for thousands of nomi-

---

[10] B. F. Westcott, *Social Aspects of Christianity* (New York: The Macmillan Company, 1900), p. 12.

[11] Quoted by A. R. Vidler, in *Christian Belief* (New York: Charles Scribner's Sons, 1950), pp. 32-33.

nal Christians in our time because they have never learned how to ask the questions to which the symbols and concepts are the answers. Our preaching may appear to some of our listeners as if we were reciting the correct solutions in the back of an arithmetic book. There is nothing wrong with the answers, and our listeners may be lulled into security by our eloquent recital of them. But to expose the learner to the agony of wrestling with the problems, the answers withheld until there is a cry for them—that involves pedagogic discipline of a high order. Yet it was God's way of teaching his covenant people. There must be a hunger and thirst for righteousness before the offer of salvation can be other than what Dietrich Bonhoeffer warns us is "cheap grace."

These matchless chapters of Genesis, then, set the scene for the majestic drama of redemption to follow. The actors are on the stage. Man is in rebellion. He is the godlet who has discovered that he has been created in the image of God and presumes upon his powers. His Creator sets bounds to that presumption. Man is exiled from the garden of Eden. But, as the drama unfolds, the same Creator who has been compelled to turn himself into Lawgiver and Judge, reveals himself as at the same time loving Father, as Lover and Saviour, as Shepherd seeking for the very ones whom he has been forced to drive into exile. God's great adventure of creating man in his own image is going to cost him dear. The gift of freedom which he has daringly bestowed and which man has employed to break the bond of trust and obedience prevents the Creator from employing the methods of power and compulsion to reestablish the relationship. God must humble himself to become the Wooer in a love story. He, Maker of heaven and earth, must, in the climactic act of wooing his bride, become a slave in the service of his own creature man and die upon a cross.

But this nuptial drama begins, as it were, with a divorce. Without an understanding of how it all began, and of what it once cost Deity to win the love of man, the revelation of the Biblical drama loses its meaning. Without Genesis and the Fall, no Gospel of Cross and Resurrection. Is there, then, a more fitting theme for setting the scene for the Lenten remembrances of the suffering of the Son of God in a garden and on a hill outside Jerusalem than the story of another garden in which the drama leading to the Cross had its fateful beginning?

These three Pre-Lenten Sundays and weeks, the Penumbra of Lent, have proved precious to our fathers in the faith as they read and reread the pages of Holy Scripture in which Creation and Fall were called to remembrance in preparation for the joy of repentance of Lent and Passiontide. May they, on occasion at least, become precious to us and our people, also.

CHAPTER FOUR

Preaching In Lent

BY WILLIAM H. NES

SINCE THIS BOOK is concerned with liturgical preaching, it is concerned with that kind of preaching which is done in church, on Sundays, within the context of Christian worship and within the context of the liturgical year. This is very obvious, to be sure, and it is not something which we have just now discovered. On the contrary, it is something we have always known; and when we say it to ourselves, we may very likely suppose that to think about it will leave us very little changed, or our preaching, or the Church within its own life and in its witness to the world. If liturgical preaching purported only some particularity of technique, some minor distinction in sermon composition, some contemporary fad of "churchmanship," it would scarcely deserve even passing attention. But it has a wider context and orientation and leads us to fresh insight into the function of the sermon in its relation to Christian worship.

The "wider orientation" is, obviously, the liturgical revival. This is something by no means peculiarly Anglican, though amongst us it has causes and goals which are pertinent to our own situation. Writing of what is now broadly known as "the Liturgical Movement," Ernest Koenker, after speaking of the Roman, Anglican, Lutheran and other "liturgical" churches, says: "Even in the United States, where liturgical movements can show slight results, hardly a single Protestant denomination has remained completely unaffected by the new thought and practice." [1] It may be said that for Anglicans the main interest is the restoration of the Eucharist as the normal worship of the congregation on the Lord's Day. This, of course, involves the extrication of the effort from the tension of "churchmanship," and to accomplish this there must be, I would suggest, from both sides of the little iron curtain in our midst, some fresh consideration of the meaning of the sacrificial character of the Eucharist, of the relation between ministerial priesthood and the corporate priesthood of the Church, and of the significance of the fact that for most of the history of the Church, and for most Christians in the world even now, the Eucharistic Liturgy has been and is the normal Christian worship of the Lord's Day. I think there will come from this, if only as something "experiential" (and perhaps something more deeply "existential") the recognition that the Eucharist is the adequate expression of Christian worship, far beyond the capacities of any other vehicle; and that this is so because

1. it is the unique focus of divine action and human response;

2. it demands, throughout its action climaxed in com-

[1] Ernest B. Koenker, *The Liturgical Renaissance in the Roman Catholic Church* (University of Chicago Press, 1954), p. v.

munion, the commitment of personal faith, and participation in the *koinonia;* and

3. it is the unique event-consciousness-response complex in which Christ is experienced by his own initiative, through faith, here and now, in together-ness.

The liturgical sermon is "the" sermon of the rubric. To speak of it at all is to give it some kind of particularity, to distinguish it from other kinds of Christian preaching. This particularity arises out of the New Testament, out of the nature of the religious situation in which the preaching is done, and out of the dual utterance of the Church in speaking to itself and speaking to the world, or rather, the dual utterance of God, to his people and to the world. What, then, is this particularity and how may we perceive it?

1. This preaching is done on Sunday, in church. As Archbishop Brilioth has remarked, the Christian sermon has a unique character because "it is a feature peculiar to the biblical religion to give to the spoken word a place in the worship of the religious community, as one of its essential elements." [2] Christian worship in its origin is the Breaking of the Bread on the first day of the week, in the assembly of the brethren. Acts 20:7 witnesses to this as an already established custom, and a century later Justin speaks of the address of "the president" as an integral part of the rite.

2. It is an address to Christians in immediate association with the lections from Holy Scripture and constitutes a part of the ministry of the Word *within* the Church. It

[2] Yngve Brilioth, *Landmarks In the History of Preaching* (the Donellan Lectures, Dublin, 1949) (London: S.P.C.K., 1950), p. 2.

therefore does not *proclaim* the Gospel to the world. It *affirms* the Gospel among those who are already committed to it. The New Testament itself is written from this point of view and is the record of what was spoken of in the Christian communities and of the way in which it was spoken; and indeed, New Testament scholarship is increasingly attentive to the possible influence of Christian worship in molding the form of the documents.

3. The address is *ministerial*. It interprets Scripture and expounds it; it discourses of the Mystery of Christ from *within* the Mystery to those who are within; it teaches Christian faith and practice to those who accept, or are by their profession bound to accept, its authority.

4. It is *pastoral*. The power of preaching belongs to Holy Orders; yet, as Canon Charles Smyth points out, there is not only a natural relation between preaching and pastorate, but an old and wise canonical relation, making the authority to preach depend upon the cure of souls.[3] There is something so necessary to be done in pastoral preaching that if it is apologetic or evangelistic it is only so for the assurance of faith. This is the preaching that gives to the children their portion of meat in due season; and in the Eucharistic Liturgy this is done in a double aspect; for there, to use St. Augustine's striking phrase, we distribute Christ as Bread and Word.

5. It is *for the congregation as a whole, as* the Congregation of God's people. This does not mean that the sermon deals in generalities without human relevance or warmth.

[3] Charles Smyth, *The Art of Preaching* (London: S.P.C.K., 1940), p. 4.

What it does require is that the preacher should *see* the congregation and understand what it is.

6. The point just made becomes clearer when we perceive that the liturgical sermon is for *edification*. Now this is a word become so individualistic in its meaning as to obscure its Biblical meaning, which is to build up the Church. Here again the Eucharist is a focus, for we are one Body because we eat of one Bread and we are begotten by the one Word to be a kind of first-fruits of God's creatures. The Church is altogether other than a mere collection of individuals, however they may be individually "edified."

7. The liturgical sermon is governed by the Christian Mystery, spoken from faith to faith. There is one Mystery of Christ and its spectrum is manifold in the beauty of its colors. If you have not recently followed this word, mystery, with your concordance through the New Testament, I am sure you will find much that is rewarding by doing so. In the liturgical action the Mystery is present and operative, and therefore the sermon must be governed by the Action of which it is a part. In the liturgical year the Mystery is entered into far more deeply than by a merely mnemonic device, and we must help our people not only to remember what God has done and revealed but to live in it.

Such considerations as these, and indeed, the New Testament itself, oblige us to recognize more clearly that there are *two* ministries of the Word. One is within the Church, the other is *from* the Church to the world. Both speak the Gospel but they speak it diversely. The one that accompanies a worship in which only Christians can take part is an utterance from God which the world cannot receive. The other is a proclamation and an invitation. Our Lord himself initiates the distinction between his disciples and others, not because the disciples were anywhere near perfect, nor yet because they were incapable of denying him as Peter did or betraying him as Judas did. To them it is given to know the Mysteries of the Kingdom and to them is given the most severe admonition and rebuke. The Epistles address as "saints" those whom they warn from the commonest human sins. The liturgical sermon, therefore, is wholly governed by what this assembly is in which the Word is here being ministered: it is the *Ecclesia Kuriake*, the Gathered of the Lord, engaged in the supreme activity of its corporate life. And since the Church is the worshipping community it must be conformed to its worship. This is the work of the Holy Spirit, who formed Christ in Mary and forms him in the Church and causes men to hear the Father's Word. By the Holy Scriptures the Word is made audible to man; and by the ministry of his servants he is made audible to men in their several generations, to those who are in the Church that they may be conformed to their membership in Christ as well as to those who are not in it that they may come to the Marriage Supper of the Lamb.

However, at this point in our discussion we are bound to face a situation—and the situation presents a quandary concerning the kind of preaching we do on Sundays in church—which confronts us at every time, and most characteristically in Lent. We have before us a congregation of so mixed a composition that we may perhaps wonder whether the liturgical sermon, if it has the features I have

enumerated, is sufficiently relevant. There are people here
who are only slightly, if at all, committed to Christ; some of
them have a very casual notion of "belonging to a church";
some are not baptized, and many are neither confirmed nor
ready and willing to be confirmed; some are more or less
lapsed communicants. So the span of the "congregation" is
all the way from serious and devout Christians to religious
window-shoppers. Obviously, this is a situation which arises
out of something inevitable and something historical and
sociological. What is inevitable is that in any congregation
the members will be, as they always have been, in different
stages of spiritual maturity. Historically, the Church is
divided, and every fragment, however it may repudiate the
soft impeachment, assumes the appearance of a denomination. To a considerable extent these denominations are
ethnic and sociological stratifications; and in this country
where Christian denominationalism is at a maximum, there
is a large part of the population that has no contact with
churches, has had no religious education, and is quite convinced that church institutionalism has no necessary connection with religion. This part of the population is now
much smaller than it formerly was, but it is still half the
nation. We should be glad if some of them find their way
into our churches, though the proclamation of the Gospel,
in any genuine evangelism, must meet them beforehand.

Now what shall we do, and especially in Lent and at
Easter when more people come to church than at any other
time? Surely we must speak to communicants, we must
speak to the Church as here in being and engaged in its own
most interior action, the worship of the Most High God;

for here the Church looks back to Baptism, inward to its being the One Body by the One Bread, upward to the present work of the One High Priest, and forward to the Day of the Lord to which the whole Creation moves. Whoever is present will hear the Church confess itself in its imperfection and in its yearning. He cannot possibly suppose that this is a forum for the general topic of religion. If the Church is reminded of what it is, of what belongs to its service and to its peace, that it possesses the promise and the blessing and stands under judgment precisely because it is the Church, a man can know what Christianity is. It is doubtful, moreover, that anybody comes into a church who has not some disposition to be a Christian; and if the New Testament has converting power, as certainly millions can testify, it is because anyone who reads it is admitted to listen in on a Christian conversation.

Although one cannot say that the liturgical sermon belongs to Lent above all other times, yet perhaps one may say that in Lent the need of it in its proper character and purpose is peculiarly conspicuous. Lent prepares the Church to partake in the Paschal Mystery and not merely to remember it. Over the gate of Lent are written, so to speak, the words "Christ our Passover is sacrificed for us"; and beneath them, to direct our preparation, we read "If ye then be risen with Christ, seek those things that are above where Christ sitteth on the right hand of God." Historically, the liturgical year has evolved out of the Christian Passover, and the Paschal Mystery dominates it as it does the Creed and the Liturgy and the structure of the Gospels. All Lenten piety is directed towards Easter; and preaching in

Lent, when it accompanies and forms a part of Christian worship, must be similarly directed. Is it not possible that many Christian people may think of Easter as the *end* of Lent rather than the *goal?* The first thing, therefore, to say about preaching in Lent is that it must be coherent with the unfolding Mystery of Christ. If this is left out of sight, and if in particular Good Friday and Easter are not seen to govern the whole meaning and movement of Lent, the preaching will be deprived of precisely that relevance which it should have. It will, as everything does when its true organizing principle disappears, become desultory and fragmentary. Many of us, I am sure, have felt this disappointment in our own preaching and the more so as we have seen our own shortcomings reflected in the state of our congregations.

This will have been a good catharsis for us when we address ourselves to the splendid alternative. Here is a parish that knows what it is, a whole portion of the People of God. Nobody can frequent its worship, nobody can participate in its activities, nobody can accept its pastoral ministry without being constantly confronted with the grandeur and demandingness of this. The people know what they do in their worship; they do not suppose that they are the spectators of a clerical thaumaturgy, or participants in a formal and external ceremony, or are present only to "make their communions" individually; they are learning more and more what it is to make Eucharist. They have been cured of any illusion that Christians need not read the Bible or cannot possibly understand it if they do. They are growing in their understanding of the Mystery of Christ as it is unfolded in the liturgical year and growing, too, in experiencing the reality of the great Feasts. To be Christian is becoming to them so different from what they had perhaps at one time imagined "church membership" to mean that it almost startles them with its new outlook on their life in the world. They have discovered that they are dealing with God and not merely with religion. Hearing the Mystery of Christ in the Church, they learn why it must be proclaimed in the world, and why the preaching of the Faith must mean the extension of the Church. For surely, unless all we have just said is a farce and a lie, the Gospel is not for you if it is not for me; and how shall we preach the Gospel to anyone whom we will not admit to our company on the same terms on which we were admitted?

This is the end of our ministering towards the household of God, that the Church may be the Church.

> The Lord shall record it, when he writeth up the peoples: lo, in Sion were they born.
> The singers also and trumpeters shall make answer: All my fresh springs are in thee. (Ps. 87:6–7)

Because Lent is a time of spiritual and bodily discipline leading to a more worthy partaking in the Mystery of the Passion and Resurrection of Our Lord, Lent is peculiarly suited to speaking within the splendid pictures of Biblical typology. We move mystically towards that "Exodus which he should accomplish at Jerusalem." Because the Church is Israel, it inherits the blessing, the admonitions, and the judgments of God's People in the Old Testament.

True, the gates of Hell shall not prevail against the Church; true, the Church is the Body, the Bride, and the Temple, and this is not something other than the visible, historic community; yet *who* will sit down to the Marriage Supper of the Lamb in that New Jerusalem where nothing enters that "maketh a lie"? If Paul might be a castaway, so might you or I. By Christians the Body of Christ is pierced, disfigured, and spit upon. "Ah, holy Jesus, how hast Thou offended? . . . Who was the guilty? Who brought this upon Thee?"

This is where we begin—on Ash Wednesday. Here we begin to walk towards the Hill of Calvary. Speaking of the "shattering realism" of the Gospel, James S. Stewart says: "It gazes open-eyed at the most menacing and savage circumstance that life can show. . . . It thrusts Golgotha upon men's vision and bids them look at that." [4] Yes; and it thrusts it on the Church's vision. The Reproaches on Good Friday strike our ears at the threshold of Lent; and *we* know that he died for us because, being the kind of people we would be but for his grace and the kind of people we are despite his grace, we are sufficient to cause his Crucifixion. And this is not only as individual sinners. No; it was *Israel* that crucified him, and we are Israel. Not all of Israel rejected him, for our Lady was a Jew and the Apostles; so not all of the Church will ever reject him. But *who* that is in Israel will and how much of Israel can in any generation? Why must it be that no person in the Church is exempted from the humiliation of Ash Wednesday—neither prelate,

[4] James S. Stewart, *Heralds of God* (New York: Charles Scribner's Sons, 1946), p. 33.

priest, or layman? Because, God save us!, it *could* be that in any generation *all* could forsake him. Think of it: even those

> who were once enlightened, and have tasted of the heavenly gift, and were made partakers of the Holy Ghost, And have tasted the good word of God, and the powers of the world to come (Heb. 6:4–5).

Therefore, it is not only Golgotha that must be thrust before our eyes, but the Empty Tomb. If we are risen with Christ—and we are—how can the Church be so much contemned in the world, not because it is Christian but because it seems so little Christian? This we must speak of on Ash Wednesday. And if we are preaching in the Liturgy, we are in that Action where, once having been enlightened in Baptism, and empowered in Confirmation, and by both Sacraments made partakers of the Holy Ghost, we are now about to receive again the Heavenly Gift, wherein also we do really taste the powers of the world to come. This is *why* we must repent and seeking God's mercy and forbearance, turn again to the "first works."

Before going on to project our preaching on the Sundays in Lent, we must consider its relation to the lections. To say that the sermon must invariably be drawn from them —from the Epistle and the Gospel or from one of the two —is, it seems to me, too inflexible in its demand. The "whole Catholic Church of Christ" (in the phrase of the 1662 Preface) is governed in Lent by the one Paschal Mystery, but it is not and has not everywhere been governed by the same liturgical lections. In all our Lenten preaching we must seek to assist our people in their (I do not know how else to speak of it) *existential* sharing in the Lord's Resurrection and in a genuine conformation of their lives to his Passion and Rising, to the praise of God the Father. If in our prayerful discretion we see a way to direct our preaching to some fresh unfolding of the Mystery without immediate reference to the lections on any Sunday, surely we may do so. This must be said for the safeguarding of our preaching from any stiff formality of identical pattern from week to week and year to year. But having said it, we must remind ourselves of what is signified in the close proximity of the sermon to the lections; for in the Eucharistic Action on a particular day the Church is making a response to the Word of God read and expounded on that particular day. This is the bond of the *synaxis*, that which binds in one action the Service of the Word and the Service of the Table. Each liturgical Gospel is a kind of *pericope* of the whole Gospel, the revelation of Christ in *these* words and in *this* deed; and each epistle or lesson is a particular illumination of the whole life of the Church. By mere cleverness a preacher may impose on the Collect, Epistle, and Gospel a singleness of subject which they do not have and which the history of their selection in the Western Church should be sufficient to warn him against. In this selection the mutual reference of Epistle and Gospel is rarely such as to warrant an attempt to treat them together in the same sermon. It is possible, however—on some Sundays more than others —when preaching from the Gospel to find in the Epistle, by reference to it as a whole and to some sentence in particular, a light cast on what the Christian response should be to the Gospel. Therefore, I shall do this when I offer to you a projected sequence of sermons through Passion Sunday.

In the Gospels for the first three Sundays we have a sequence in which, in each one, evil is encountered and defeated. Now what is the reality of these encounters? "But surely, Reverend, you don't believe in a personal Devil." Well, but evidently Jesus did—unless by an overexuberant application of form-criticism all that he is alleged to have said is the projection of what the first Christians thought he might have said. Or, if he did believe in the Devil and imagined himself to be in a conflict with him, is this the dispensable costume of the Incarnation? For myself, I have no doubt that part of the reason why Christianity appears so irrelevant to so much of the modern world is because human life has shrunk to be a merely planetary phenomenon, and nothing is either as deep or as high, as dark or as bright as the Scriptures represent it to be. When you stand up to preach on the Temptation, you must say what conflict *there* took place: where was the evil—in *him*, in his own thoughts, wishes, "conditioning," "Messianic complex"? When you preach on the third Sunday, who or what is the "strong man armed," a symbol? A symbol of *what?*

The Paschal Mystery is the Mystery of Christ's victory, and of ours through him and in him. Throughout Lent this must be before us as we follow the Captain of our salvation. It is a great battle and it has a great end which is the restoration of all things in him. With us are Michael and his host and a great company of just men not to be made perfect without us. In the world we have tribulation and tempest and warfare. Lent, far from hiding this, compels us to face it. But we are already "come unto mount Sion and to the city of the living God" because we are raised in Christ and are of his Body, of his flesh and of his bones. From the world's standpoint this is at best but a paradox; for the Church it is a Mystery, something revealed and something one can really live in. Yet one does not come to live in it merely by the exercise of the imagination. It is the work in the praying Christian of the Holy Ghost, and *this* is what preaching must say. In every Eucharist the reality is *given* and on Easter, which is the Lord's Day that makes all other Lord's Days, it is *given*. This is no fragmentary or piece-meal giving; but because in this life we live in *successive-ness*, day by day and year by year, our life is yet, when it is done, but a day, and our Father gives us our daily bread.

And now, as I project a sermon-sequence through Passion Sunday, I do not presume to intrude into your sermon-making by offering sermon outlines. Much less do I suggest that something much better cannot be evolved in a hundred different ways. What I am offering is designed simply to illustrate certain specific concerns of the liturgical sermon in Lent. It will be fuller for the first Sunday than for the others.

THE FIRST SUNDAY

Our Lord's Temptation very properly confronts us at the beginning of Lent, for it was the beginning of that public road that took him to the Cross. It is the prelude and presage of his Passion as well as the climax of testing following his Baptism and the profound meditation of all the thirty "silent years." Here is the onslaught of the "mystery of lawlessness" to challenge him in his mission and in his Person. The challenge is to man as man, not only in his need for food and his compulsion to hazard under providence, but in the direction of his power; for though man has not absolute power he has real power. Having none, he would have no real temptation. He has power over nature, he has power to hazard and to dare, and his history is traced in the building and the ruin of his kingdoms. But he must do and he must act, because he can. Now because Christ is Man—The Man—he is tempted in the core and marrow of all-inclusive temptation. It strikes at the very pitch of his self-knowledge and of his knowledge of what he has come into the world for. This is no painted ship upon a painted ocean, this temptation, no Docetic play-acting. This was travail and conflict, a confrontation in the ultimate dimension of evil. We do well not to paraphrase his answer, for no man reading the Gospel narrative can miss the rugged majesty and simplicity of its import.

Our Lord's Deity is not something *beside* his humanity, but incarnate in it. In the same way, the divine mystery of the Temptation is not something beside or in addition to the tempting of the Son of Man. Rather, because Jesus is Christ and Only-begotten, the Temptation of Jesus is for us a curtain drawn to reveal the horizon of the Passion. The Enmity that crucified the Lord of Glory is an enmity deeper and darker than man's; that negation, that repudiation, which confronts the Power, Justice, and Love of God is indeed in man and nevertheless, unless the New Testament is altogether wrong, enslaves him beyond his apprehension. This is why, when they crucified him, they knew not what they did. We never know—yet we do it. Since, then, as St. Leo said, God did not will to redeem our nature apart from it, Christ took our nature "for it became him, for whom are all things, and by whom are all things, in bringing many sons unto glory, to make the captain of their salvation perfect through sufferings" (Heb. 2:10). This temptation was one of those sufferings, for you and for me. When you see him on the Cross, you see what happened to a Man who would worship only God. But you see something beyond this. You see the obedience of the Eternal Son within the Godhead and the eschatological issue of the Incarnation, for "when all things shall have been subdued unto him, then shall the Son also himself be subject unto him that did put all things under him that God may be all in all" (I Cor. 15:28). This is the decision of the Temptation—that God may be all in all.

Our Lord's temptation was concerned with bread, with God's sovereign providence, and with God's kingdom. These are our needs: for without bread a man cannot live on the earth, without the direction and protection of God his life is not worth living, and God's kingdom embraces every splendor of which man is capable and for which he was created. Our Lord, too, in his humanity, which he took for our sakes, needed bread, but he said that bread alone, without God's Word, is not enough to sustain life—animal life, yes, but not a *man's* life. Our Lord, too, in his human life, lived under the direction and sovereignty of his Father, as we must. He came to win a kingdom and to be its King, but on no other terms than his Father's. We have now listened to his Word. We are about to offer our bread, which God has given us, not to feed God but for him to feed us by it with the Living Bread; and when we offer it, we offer our alms that Christ's brothers and ours may not

be hungry while we are full. Do you not see and understand?—Christ is here, the Bread and the Word, in the one
Person, in the one ministration to us. God's providence has
overshadowed us and is with us in his Son and the continuous indwelling of the Holy Spirit. All that his providence
does and can do for us is here in the Redemption which we
celebrate and in which we partake. Because Christ is in the
midst of us, his kingdom is in the midst of us, and being in
him, we are in it. All this Christ has given us; all this he
gives us in every Eucharist. He can give it because he won
it. By all our Eucharists, one by one, we move towards our
death, as he moved from his Birth, from his Temptation, to
his own Death. Since every day we move towards death,
how shall we move?—flogged like a galley-slave to his
dungeon by biological certainty?—or by many Thanksgivings, in a life of thanksgiving and trust because by
Christ's Resurrection we are sure of our own?

But even a life of thanksgivings is not a primrose path.
Why should I think that if I am in Christ I should expect to
be unassailed by temptation? He was tempted, the Captain.
Who am I, the meanest soldier of the line, to think God
unkind if I must battle temptation? Lent is a training-time
for inescapable Christian warfare. Today I am again fur-
nished for it. "We, then, as workers together with him,
beseech you that ye receive not the grace of God in vain
. . . behold now is the day of salvation." Today is another
beginning for us of dealing with ourselves as the children
of God, and as members of Christ, and as inheritors of the
kingdom of God. This is why we must give no offense. Not
only must Paul be alert that the "ministry be not blamed."

We must strive, also, and for the same reason, for each of us has his ministry in the Body of Christ and each in his own order: Paul the Apostle and you the layman, for we are all one kingdom and one priesthood, that the kingdom and the power and the glory may be God's, because they *are* his. How long shall God's name be blasphemed among the nations because we, who are his people, serve him more audibly with our lips than in our lives? Pray, brethren, that when Easter comes we may be found entering in, by the golden gate of a Christian life, to that glorious Resurrection of which even today we are made partakers.

THE SECOND SUNDAY

In the Prayer Book rite, the Gospel today is the episode of the Syro-Phoenician woman. For comparison: the Roman lection is Matt. 17, The Transfiguration; the Orthodox have Mark 2, the healing of the paralytic. It is possible, therefore, to say the Christian thing suitable to this Sunday without being confined to a single Scripture. However, our own selection says something of great import for this Sunday. Our Lord, having defeated the onslaught of evil upon himself, proceeds in the launching of his ministry to rescue men and women from its power. The needs of human beings for rescue from evil are universal in all societies; but there is also a specific character of the demonic in history that it takes forms specifically endemic to particular societies and cultures and becomes epidemic in them. I once heard an experienced doctor say that there are people in institutions and hospital beds that only world peace can cure. Surely Christians must become aware that, with all our technical advantage in the treatment of disease, we are beset with over-all infections that only the power of Christ can heal.

Yet there is more significance in this Gospel. This woman was a Gentile. Here is the beginning, by Jesus himself, of that ministry to Gentiles that breaks down the wall of partition and makes it possible for Gentiles to rejoice with his people, for they are the "other sheep" whom he must bring. In this Eucharist let us look back to our own Baptism, who by nature were not the seed of Abraham. Christ makes nobodies to be somebodies; and we who were alien from the commonwealth of Israel are now seated with Abraham and Isaac and Jacob in the kingdom of God.

And further: the "children's bread" is conspicuous in this Gospel. If the children refuse the bread and the feast, they are cast out; and if the "dogs" humbly accept the crumbs under the table, they become the children. The tension of the Old Testament in the Old Israel can as well be the tension in the New Israel; and in epitome it lies in this—whether God belongs to us or we to God. There are among the things quite clear in Scripture, these: (1) that Israel is the elect people and that the wall of partition is cast down, not for the dissolution of Israel but for its potentially universal expansion; and (2) that status is no protection against the inexorable moral realism of God's judgment, for God, even of the stones, can raise up children to Abraham. Those of us who are Episcopalians sometimes display a singular broad-mindedness about other people's religion —or lack of any, and this brings us the convenient reward of not having to bother about being missionary. Today we eat of the children's bread. Let us remember that we must live as God's children; and let us remember, too, what Jesus said to his disciples concerning the multitude, "Give ye them to eat." Consider also the Epistle. How can we bring the Gentiles to the knowledge of God if we live as Gentiles who know not God?

THE THIRD SUNDAY

Again, it is impossible to evade what is for our time the "problem of the demonic in the New Testament," yet the emphasis is not on the demonic but on the victory of Christ. Christianity is not a dualism. It does not see an eternal and unresolved conflict of good and evil. The kingdom of evil is a divided, self-frustrating thing. It can, however, ruin a man, and ruin his society. It can even taint the Church with its own infection so that in the name of Christ the Church can do to those whom it regards as its enemies the very same things that anti-Christian states do to Christians. In this Gospel Jesus makes it clear that the two kingdoms are absolutely irreconcilable. In him and in his miracles the kingdom of God is here. If you can't see good in the healing of this man here before you, where will you ever see it? Can evil cast out evil? Evil has power to propagate evil, but it can never undo evil.

Today the Mystery of God's kingdom dominates our path to Good Friday and Easter. Today we see "the Mighty One robbing the Prince of evil of his authority, and spoiling his goods" [5]; yet today we know that before

---

[5] Edwyn C. Hoskyns, "The Christ of the Synoptic Gospels," in *Essays Catholic and Critical* (New York: The Macmillan Company, 1926), p. 172.

the Mighty One loomed still Gethsemane and the Cross.
Thus, as we share in the Mystery of Christ, we find revealed both the predicament and the victory of Christian
life in this present world.

> If we ask which is the dominant note in this petition
> [of the Lord's Prayer: "Thy Kingdom come"] the
> answer is unquestionably the future. We cannot get rid
> of "come." We are still at this point thinking of God
> and not of ourselves, praying that He will finish His
> work. But I find it impossible rigorously to separate
> future and present. In this time between the times the old
> idea of taking the yoke of the kingdom upon us retains
> all its force, and concern for the final coming is surely
> unreal unless we are trying to fit ourselves for it by
> making the Lord King of our lives now.[6]

THE FOURTH SUNDAY

In "this time between the times" Refreshment Sunday
gives a special and precious meaning to our Eucharist today,
and for our refreshment the Epistle most aptly supplements
the Gospel. In *this* time the predicament and victory of
Christian life—the kingdom coming and already come;
the evident and present conflict of the two kingdoms in our
society and each man's life; the apparent disjunction of
power and love bringing with it the apparent enigma of
justice—confronts us with an intellectual paradox that only
the experience of Resurrection, received by faith, can il-
lumine and resolve.

The Eucharist is the food of wayfarers. In anyone un-
wearied by the spiritual combat of life, in anyone who finds

[6] John Lowe, *The Interpretation of the Lord's Prayer* (the Hale
Memorial Sermon) (Evanston: Seabury-Western Theological Seminary,
1955), p. 15.

the world good enough to satisfy his hunger, there is no desire for refreshment. The Beatitude is for those who hunger after righteousness. Yet not only of man's spiritual nature must a Christian voice speak. Although the Feeding of the Five Thousand is an anticipation of the Eucharist and of the eschatological Messianic Banquet, it is in compassion on the people lest they should faint in the wilderness. Poverty, weariness, and oppression are not things in which Christ is concerned only for their analogy with spiritual conditions. The Gospel speaks today of food, and the Epistle of freedom, which only in God's kingdom can be truly had. By this Eucharist we have the feeding and enter by faith into the liberation in "Jerusalem which is above" and are refreshed, *from* the weariness of previous spiritual combat, *for* the travail of the Passion, *looking to* the Resurrection, *by* the Living Bread.

PASSION SUNDAY

The altered tone of Lent today is sounded in the Epistle. This alteration is indeed one more of tonality than of theme; for hitherto the Mystery of Christ has been no less dominant than in what now follows, and likewise our response to him and participation in him, which has been spoken in the Epistles hitherto, is not silenced; yet there is a difference profound and moving, like a change of orchestration. The Epistle today speaks wholly of Christ and his Sacrifice. The altercation in the Gospel presages and precipitates the Passion; for they said that he who casts out devils has a devil; and when he said "Before Abraham was, I am," they took up stones to cast at him. Who are *they?*

They are Israel, God's people. When he who is the meaning and fulfilment of their law, their prophets, and their worship, declares himself, they wish only to stone him; and their high priest, as the head and figure of the people to recognize and receive him, delivers him to Pilate for crucifixion. In this, Israel is the epitome and figure of mankind in "man's resistance against reuniting love, his estrangement from himself, from other beings, and from the ground of his being." [7]

Yet we must never speak only, or even chiefly, of the blackness of human sin or of the tragedy of the Passion. Indeed, tragedy itself is something other and different from pessimism. No; we must always speak of the Passion in relation to the Resurrection; we must always speak of sin in relation to grace and the power of Christ's sacrifice. If we do not, we belie what the Lord said of his own death. Today, as we enter into the Passion, we enter into the mighty deed by which God has redeemed the world. This is the Mystery known to us and by us to be cried aloud,

> That in the dispensation of the fulness of times he might gather together in one all things in Christ, both which are in heaven, and which are on earth; even in him (Ephes. 1:10).

[7] Paul Tillich, *Love, Power, and Justice* (New York: Oxford University Press, 1954), p. 108.

CHAPTER FIVE

Preaching in Holy Week

BY FREDERICK C. GRANT

I

IT IS THE GLORY, not the shame, the strength, not the weakness of the Christian religion that it is a historical religion. It takes history seriously, and its beginnings are traced in a biography and a resulting historical movement, not a mythology. There are, of course, religions whose real inner substance is a metaphysical system—something which is either true or false quite regardless of historical events or the human experience of events: a metaphysical system cruising aloft, and coming down from above the clouds only for a momentary three-point landing somewhere in history (almost anywhere will do). But such a contact with history is only incidental, one might almost say accidental; the truth of the religion does not depend in the least upon its history. Buddhism is a classic example of such a religion; Gnosticism is another; Neoplatonism is another. On the contrary, Christianity is centered in history, rises out of history, depends upon a particular sequence of events within a specific historical period, and apart from this history would be not so much false as almost wholly lacking in distinctive content. Apart from the *event* of Christ, in history, Christianity is only an unrevised, unreformed type of Judaism, though Judaism also was a historical religion, distinctively different from all other cults and beliefs as a result of the Acts of God in the past, i.e., within history. It was a religion which magnified history, and transformed the old, traditional cult observances into historical commemorations: for example, the primitive spring festival of first-fruits became the Passover, commemorating Israel's divine deliverance from slavery in Egypt, a historical event. As the "fulfilment" of Judaism, of the Old Testament, of earlier prophecy, of the partial (but genuine) revelation of God "in many parts and in divers manners," Christianity was from the first a historical religion. And this remains true, regardless of the fact that some modern writers present Christianity as non-historical, i.e., as a set of doctrines or ideas or convictions for which history is irrelevant. The Church has never been able to accommodate itself to such a view—either as set forth in ancient Gnosticism or in modern philosophical idealism.

A religion which takes history seriously must face up to and fully recognize the evils in the world and in human life, and also the defeats and frustrations which are the experience of every man and woman. And this Christianity does. The scandal (in Greek, *skandalon*, i.e., "stumbling block," the cause of falling, the great impediment to belief) of the Cross was frankly acknowledged by the early Christians, especially by St. Paul, who set it in the very forefront of his preaching. As a result, Christianity is in closer contact with reality, as lived and experienced by men in all ages and everywhere, than a faith which emerges out of philosophical speculation or abstract dogma or ethical idealism severed from the harsh realities of human existence. Hence, the preaching of the "Cross of Christ." Instead of explaining away the scandal of a crucified leader, the Church found in the Cross the point at which God came to grips with the evil in the world—which centered in man's sin, man's denial of God's goodness. Among certain early Christian thinkers, including Paul, the background of man's sin included the rebellious *archontes*, the wicked powers in the heavens; but this only amplified the significance of the Cross and gave it a cosmic magnitude—as in the sixth-century Latin hymn of Venantius Fortunatus of Ravenna, describing

> the blood whose flowing streams
> Cleanse earth and ocean, stars and universe.[1]

Our first requirement, in preaching the Gospel of the Cross in Holy Week, is a complete and unfailing realism, i.e., an unflagging loyalty to truth and reality. Mere rhetoric and purple oratory should be utterly taboo, whoever the preacher! The historical principle requires us to be true to the Gospel narratives, carefully studied, compared, explained, evaluated. The spiritual principle requires us to be strictly loyal to human need and to the relevance of the Gospel to men's actual condition. Hence, no dreamy, fanciful interpretations are allowable, however appealing, however widely circulated by novelists and script writers for

[1] A. S. Walpole, *Early Latin Hymns* (New York: the Macmillan Company, 1923), p. 171. The hymn is no. 66 in *The Hymnal 1940*.

the moving pictures. We are "dying men preaching the message of life to the dying." It is a message of life in and through and beyond death—a message of hope and assurance; we cannot trifle with day-dreams. In saying this, I am aware that even the most orthodox views are sometimes presented as if they were based upon a kind of pious mythology, unreal and irrelevant. It is even proposed that the stories in the apocryphal gospels of the second, third, and fourth centuries should be taken seriously, e.g., such a pious legend as the one which affirms that the Blessed Mother of our Lord also rose from the dead, or that her body was assumed into heaven. By others the libels of unscrupulous adversaries of Christianity are accepted, e.g., that Jesus was the son of a German soldier and a Jewish girl in Nazareth; or that he was a jobless carpenter who went to Egypt looking for work and there learned tricks of magic, returned to Galilee, and overawed his old neighbors with his "miracles." The uncritical acceptance of such later embroideries upon the Gospel story—whatever their motivation, whether pious devotion or malicious hatred of the Christian name—is utterly incompatible with the preaching of the Gospel. The acceptance of such tales, even their serious consideration, reflects the quality of mind we are producing today, when long and improbable historical novels or fantastic moving pictures have taken the place of genuine history for hundreds of thousands, perhaps millions, of ordinary people.

Must we then begin with a critical examination of the sources for the history of Holy Week? Certainly! But not in the pulpit. The preacher should have made his historical research long before he prepares his sermon. To do otherwise would be to act like a surgeon who began an operation with a lecture on anatomy: quite appropriate in the Medical School, but not in the operating room with a patient's life in the balance. We have all heard of the professor who explained to his students the theory of the Gospel source "Q" but "failed to confront them with Jesus Christ"; but certainly the confrontation with Jesus Christ depends in some measure upon the convictions reached by the preacher as to the historical reality of the sources behind the Gospels. And there is a place for both the historical research and the faithful proclamation of the Gospel message. Nevertheless we hear it said that the most effective preachers of the Gospel are the old-fashioned kind who disregard modern historical and literary criticism, who take the Bible "just as it is" (usually the King James Version), and proceed to interpret it upon the basis of their own religious, moral, and spiritual experience. To them it is a "saving" word. Of course! And it is a tragedy if we who value historical research and are driven by our very conscience to seek out the original meaning of the Scriptures, i.e., what the words meant to the writers and first readers of the Gospels, should fail to find here the "saving" word to proclaim to men and women in their need. But this does not necessarily follow. As a matter of fact, it ought not to follow. For the most careful historical and literary analysis of the Gospels should bring us face to face with the situation in which the Gospels arose, in which the Gospel-tradition was handed down, and in which it originated. For the men who risked their lives to proclaim the message contained in the Gospels and in the New Testament as a whole were in the closest contact with both historical reality and human need. They were not leisurely philosophers attending a discussion club devoted to new ideas—like those described in Acts 17. They were not readers of select chapters in the latest historical work, gathered for afternoon tea and a literary hour at Pliny's villa. They were men headed for the arena or the lion or a cross in Nero's gardens. When we get the New Testament into proper historical focus—and skill is required to make the delicate adjustment—it becomes clear that no other method is tolerable in dealing with such precious, life-giving records. "Criticism" does not mean adverse or antagonistic "criticizing of the Bible." It is an ancient and honorable word in Biblical study, and means simply "evaluation," "judgment" (Greek *krisis*), i.e., the expert decision of the case as between rival views and interpretations, the meaning of certain difficult words, or the true text as opposed to variant readings in different manuscripts. When one has been engaged in such studies for most of a lifetime, perhaps he may be permitted to testify: Criticism does not destroy faith; it supports and strengthens it. And as against allegorism, or modernism—i.e., the reading of one's own views, or of popular modern views, into the sacred text—criticism is indispensable and far safer.[2]

But this does not mean that every reader must be a Biblical critic! Nor does it even mean that everyone must accept the "findings" of the Biblical critics. We all live in a complex universe of intersecting spheres, and we must

[2] On this use of "modernism" see E. C. Colwell, *The Study of the Bible* (the University of Chicago Press, 1937), Ch. 4; F. C. Grant, *How to Read the Bible* (New York: Morehouse-Gorham, 1956), esp. Ch. 6.

recognize that one man's sphere of interests and of understanding need not be the same as his neighbor's. For example, there are persons who have almost no interest whatsoever in history—at least not in the history prior to 1776
or at the most 1492. When you refer to some event or
condition or personage in the ancient world, they are not
able to fit it into any pattern of reference; it might just as
well be a chapter out of a fairy tale—equally real, equally
unreal, since anything might possibly have happened in that
never-never land of the faraway past. There are also persons
who have no interest in science; for them science means
only gadgets, telephones, aeroplanes, radios, and now
atomic bombs, with the possibility of interplanetary travel
someday before long. They have never caught a glimpse
of the scientific view of the world, of the vast unimaginable
sweep of universal evolution from the birth of a galaxy to
the birth of a human child. The uniformity of nature, even
a relative uniformity, which is now the prevailing view,
means nothing to them; anything might happen, anything
may have happened in the past, for their world is the pic-
turesque world of science fiction or of the medieval geog-
raphers. To such persons, the Gospel-narratives set no
problems, and—let me add—such persons should not be
required to face them; for they have neither the material
for the making of the problems nor the material for their
solution. There are tens of thousands of such persons all
around us today, even in this "scientific" age. But the fact
that they are not troubled by historical or scientific problems does not leave them any less in need of the message
of the Gospel. The intersecting spheres of thought in which

they live and move and think merely happen to be different from those of some other men, including many of the clergy. Unless we can bridge the hiatus between the two types of thinking, honestly and without "trimming," we shall never be able to preach to ordinary people as we should. There is no suggestion in the Gospels that those who hold a non-historical, non-scientific view of the world are going to be excluded from the kingdom of Heaven! But neither should *they* try to force their non-critical views upon others, though this is often attempted. One wonders how it fares with the oncoming generation, caught in the cross-fire of argument—over the Bible or its interpretation, or the earliest Christian history, or the present-day doctrines of the Church and their proper formulation. What do they make of it, especially when religion is identified with antiquated views, untenable to anyone who has accepted the modern scientific outlook even in a small degree? To many persons, no doubt, the easiest solution of the conflict is to reject or at least to bypass religion altogether. Of course, religion is not theology, however necessary theology may be in some circles—or "spheres"; religion means faith and worship and a way of living, which for us Christians means the way of love. But the historical questions will not be side-tracked. For it does make a difference that Jesus Christ lived and died in Palestine nineteen centuries ago; and it makes a difference what kind of person he was, how he lived, why he died. This requirement brings us close to the message of Holy Week.

One or two inferences follow at once: If we are to preach the Gospel of Holy Week in terms of utter realism, as real as the Gospels and their sources; in terms of the human situation as it existed in the first century; in terms of man's continual deepest need, which God himself met and shared and solved—then every hint of unreality must be resolutely erased, no matter from which side the suggestion comes. The charming, idealized, romantic nineteenth-century figure of Christ—the "gentle prophet and seer from Nazareth" —will not do; neither will the purely theological twentieth-century conception of him. For example, the idea that as God he knew all the time that his death on the Cross was merely a role to be played, just as an actor knows that in playing King Lear or Hamlet or Macbeth he will not really die— such a portrayal is almost unadulterated Gnosticism, denounced repeatedly in the New Testament and the Creed. It was thought by many in the second century that because —as men believed—a divine being could not suffer, therefore it was necessary to maintain that Jesus did not suffer, even on the Cross. Just before the first nail was driven into his body, the spiritual Christ returned to the heavenly places, leaving a corpse to be nailed to the Cross. He knew all this in advance; therefore he planned his exodus from this world in such a way as to escape pain. The next step was to infer that he had never really suffered even hunger or thirst. Instead, his body had been only a phantom, now palpable, now impalpable. As the apocryphal Acts of John describes it,[3] this disciple testified that sometimes he put out his hand to touch Jesus and his body was real; at other times it was a wraith—as unreal and intangible as the shade of Odysseus' mother in the nether world. Undoubtedly,

---

[3] See M. R. James, *The Apocryphal New Testament* (New York: Oxford University Press, 1924), pp. 228ff., esp. §§ 89, 93.

those who held such views thought they did Christ honor, viewing his divinity as almost anyone would in the Graeco-Roman world of the first two centuries. But it made Christ unreal, and the Church as a whole opposed this new doctrine with all its might. To some persons what was taking place was instantly clear: as Ignatius of Antioch wrote to the Trallians on his way to martyrdom, "If Christ suffered merely in appearance . . . then why am *I* in bonds?" [4] Against this Gnostic interpretation the Church threw up three strong lines of defense: the apostolic creed, the apostolic writings (the New Testament), and the apostolic succession (the testimony of the Church's teachers in the great central sees of Christendom). Every phrase of the creed—basically the old Roman baptismal creed of the mid-second century but no longer confined to Rome, as Ignatius' letter shows—was designed to deny the thesis of the Docetic Gnostics. "I believe in God the Father Almighty [*Pantokratōr*, All-powerful, All-ruler], maker of heaven and earth"—God the Father was the Creator, not some inferior Aeon, the Demiurge. "And in Jesus Christ" who was "born, suffered, was crucified, died, was buried, and rose again"—every word rules out the theory that he was a temporary apparition clothed in an unreal body, a mere likeness or resemblance (*homoiōma*) of human flesh. The modern idea that the creed ought to have mentioned the Sermon on the Mount or the Beatitudes is nonsense; the purpose of the creed was to deny and repudiate the theory that threatened to destroy the whole central belief of Chris-

[4] § 10. See text and tr. in K. Lake, *The Apostolic Fathers*, in the *Loeb Classical Library*, Vol. I (1912), pp. 212ff.; cf. H. Bettenson, *Documents of the Christian Church* (new ed., New York: Oxford University Press, 1947), pp. 49f.

tianity. It even went the length of saying, "I believe in . . . the resurrection of the flesh," in order to apply to *us* the same principle of concreteness and substantiality that applied to Christ. In time the Church changed this to read, "the resurrection of the body," under the influence of Paul's teaching in I Corinthians 15; but the original phrase was the anti-Gnostic, anti-Docetic, anti-esoteric, anti-spiritualistic phrase *resurrectio carnis*. So also the Church: it was no group of conventicles of the elect, the truly "spiritual" as opposed to the "material" (*hylic*) or merely pedestrian believers: "I believe in the holy catholic church [which is] the [true] communion of saints."

This profound insistence upon historical reality, which, as Adolf Harnack said, characterized the teaching of the "Great" Church as opposed to that of the heretics, is also to be seen in the later creeds, all the way to that of Chalcedon. Jesus Christ is both truly God (*alēthōs theos*) and perfectly man (*teleiōs anthrōpos*). He is not one of these only, either God or man, to the exclusion of the other. To some persons it seemed that piety and devotion recommended that he should be viewed as completely God, not man—or man only in a diluted sense. To others, it seemed that he must be truly man, with the divine element coming down upon him, inspiring but transitory. The Church ruled otherwise: the words were carefully chosen, to preserve the balance of the faith: he was *truly* God, *completely* (i.e., perfectly) man. As Bishop Charles Gore rightly insisted many years ago in his famous Bampton Lectures,[5] the terms

[5] *The Incarnation of the Son of God* (1891). On the creeds, see Bettenson, pp. 34ff.; J. N. D. Kelly, *Early Christian Creeds* (New York: Longmans Green, 1950).

of the later ecumenical creeds were not intended as definitions but as boundary marks, affirming the open areas within which Christian thought could freely operate. As he used the figure, they marked off the "common," the open green in the middle of the old English village, which no one, prince or baron or commoner, had the right to seize and fence in. Hence it is a complete mistake to assume that we do honor to our Lord and offer him the greater glory when we picture him as incapable of either physical or mental suffering—physical agony or mental anguish. This is not the real teaching of the New Testament or of the Catholic Faith, but the contrary. He was no Gnostic Aeon who once upon a time came down to earth, was temporarily garbed in a thin but transparent garment of flesh, and then, when eventually faced with the prospect of genuine suffering and death, eluded his captors (like some Greek god on the field before Troy) and slipped away, returning to the celestial realm from which he had come. Such a theory is a complete denial of the principle of the *teleiōs anthrōpos*, the utter historical reality of Jesus' human nature.

Nor can we describe him as a weak, tired, beaten idealist who paid with his life for his temerity in rebuking the religious and political authorities of his day—a purely human Jesus whose death was only one more among the countless martyrdoms which took place whenever rebellion broke out among a subject but still restless people, like the eight hundred men crucified by Alexander Jannaeus, the two thousand crucified by Varus, the many thousands crucified by the Romans along the Judean roads during the siege and after the fall of Jerusalem, the six thousand whose crosses lined the road all the way from Capua to Rome after the great slave rebellion. Such a theory is a complete denial of the principle of the *alēthōs theos,* the truth of his divine nature, and the reality of his divine mission.

Yet who has not heard Good Friday addresses which at least tended in one direction or the other—either making Jesus so completely divine that he could not really suffer and merely played a role which he had long foreseen and accepted, or else making him so completely and exclusively human that he roused only our pity instead of awakening our faith? [6] Either extreme robs the Gospel of its power. A god who cannot suffer, who cannot come to grips with evil, who cannot die, or a man who was only one more tragic, pitiful victim of fate or circumstance, of human tyranny, jealousy, or hatred—either figure is unreal and inadequate, both as compared with the New Testament accounts of Jesus' Passion and also as measured by our human need for light upon the riddle of man's ultimate frustration and defeat in death. It is true, phrases are found here and there in the New Testament which seem to imply one or the other of these two one-sided views: for example, Paul's phrase, Christ came "in the likeness of sinful flesh" (a word which at least comforted if it did not inspire the later Gnostics); or John's expression, "Jesus, knowing that he had come from God and was going to God"; or Jesus' words foreshowing "by what death he was to die"—such language seems to justify the later idea that he did some things as God, others as man, and foreknew in detail his

---

[6] See *Christ's Victory and Ours* (New York: The Macmillan Company, 1951), p. 43; *The Passion of the King* (New York: The Macmillan Company, 1955), p. 24.

whole career from the beginning.[7] But these expressions were used either before the Docetic-Gnostic crisis had arisen (at least before its full implications were clear), or else they reflect an attempt to maintain *rapport* with Docetic ways of thinking, to use Docetic language up to a certain point, and thus maintain contact with this radical wing and if possible win back those who were tending in its direction. Certainly the language dates from a period prior to the rejection of Gnosticism in the second century. It is like the use of "Arian" language before the Arian heresy arose: perfectly orthodox writers used the term *homoiousios* before its full implications were clear!

But we must view the New Testament *as a whole*, and the early Christian faith in its totality. And the faith as a whole, the New Testament as a whole, justify the later creeds; for the entire Christian faith in its central, normative movement was headed in the direction of Nicaea and Chalcedon. For the Gospels and the Creeds alike insist upon the historical reality of our Lord's human nature. In our preaching, therefore, we must be careful not to let any suggestion of unreality escape our lips, however devout the intention behind the words! The full, complete, perfect human nature of Jesus must not be curtailed or denied; to do so means making him unreal—his sufferings, his death, his resurrection—and if unreal, then meaningless for salvation. However powerfully the scene may seem to affect us emotionally, if Jesus is not presented as truly and perfectly human the final result will be really frustrating and defeating, and it will not be the preaching of the Gospel.

[7] Rom. 8:3; Jn. 13:1, 12:33, 18:32.

There is one more point in this preliminary theological approach to the subject: we must always bear in mind the fact that the atonement or reconciliation with God is not identical with any of the various theories which have been advanced in order to explain it—or perhaps, in some cases, only to illustrate it. Behind all the theories stands the towering fact, the sublime, transcendent mystery of our reconciliation to God through Christ: "In Christ, God was reconciling the world to himself" (II Cor. 5:19). Moreover, the conception of sin which is taken for granted in the Bible is the ancient social, even biological, conception—not one of the merely forensic, juridical conceptions which prevailed in the late patristic and medieval periods, or the modern individualistic, introspective, psychological conception, for which the real problem is the removal or cancellation of guilt, or the reassurance of a troubled conscience, or relief from the gnawing anxiety that troubles most modern men. Instead, the ancient conception of sin, which is also the Biblical conception, views it as wrong-doing which results in pollution, infection, or disease, something which must be cleansed, neutralized, removed, and "put away." Here our best guide, i.e., the fullest and most explicit unfolding of the idea, both of sin and of its expiation, is the Epistle to Hebrews. It is generally recognized that the Epistle (really a homily) is a theological writing which combines a Platonic view of the world with an allegorical view of the Old Testament, much as in the Jewish Platonism of Philo of Alexandria. But it also gives us the ancient, primitive view of sin and atonement, deeply embedded in the Old Testament and in ancient religion generally, especially in the Greek religion and the Hebrew.

No other writing in the New Testament gives as full an explanation of the Church's doctrine of the Atonement—certainly the Pauline epistles do not, even though St. Paul is usually credited with formulating (or inventing!) the doctrine. Apparently, the author of Hebrews went back to a starting point prior to Paul, even the one which Paul himself presupposed as a part of the original *kērygma* or proclamation of the Gospel, which he himself had received from those in Christ before him, and which he had handed on to his first hearers in Corinth (and presumably elsewhere): "Christ died for our sins in accordance with the scriptures" (I Cor. 15:3). What mattered most was the great *fact of reconciliation;* and it could be verified in one's own experience of forgiveness. But how this new relation to God had come to pass; how sin had actually been done away with, and with it the attendant feelings of guilt; and how the "new being in Christ" had become possible—all this was hard to explain, if not indeed frankly inexplicable. Paul has a half-dozen or more metaphors which he uses in expressing, describing, or illustrating the fact, though none of them explains it:[8] it is a release from slavery, an act of adoption, a rebirth, the beginning of the new creation, a sacrifice, a coming of age, a "translation" from one realm to another—all these are metaphors, none is a "rationale" or systematic explanation. Later theologians sometimes took the metaphors as explanations, i.e., as factual statements; but they must be studied as a group, recognizing that back of them all is the prior fact of reconciliation with God and the new life in Christ. On the other hand, the author of Hebrews,

[8] See Adolf Deissmann, *Paul* (new ed., New York: George H. Doran Co., 1926), pp. 167-83.

his thought steeped in the sacrificial doctrine of the Old Testament—far more so than Paul's, whose problems were psychological and moral—turned naturally to the principle of sacrifice for an explanation; to him it was no metaphor, but concrete fact. His theory of sacrifice is the ancient piacular, expiatory, one might almost say biological, theory, according to which sin is a poisonous *miasma* infecting society (a group, a family, a city) and requiring not so much punishment as removal. This was effected first by concentration of the pollution in one individual (a thing, a person, or an animal) and then his or its removal and death or destruction (by burial, drowning, murder, or exile). At the very least, the person or thing so designated, e.g., as a *pharmakos*, must be kept out of contact with the people: he (or it) was the sin-*bearer*, i.e., the one who bore it away (Num. 18:23; Lev. 16:22; Isa. 53:6, 12; Jn. 1:29). To many later interpreters, the term "to bear" sin meant "to bear," i.e., to suffer, its penalty, or "to bear" the guilt, i.e., to suffer for another; these are juridical or legal concepts, which were natural enough in western Europe in later centuries when the practice of sacrifice had long ceased and its real meaning had been forgotten. But in the first century, and especially in eastern and southern Europe and in the Near East, the age-old connotations of sacrifice and of "sin-bearing" were still vividly conceived and felt, and the author of Hebrews senses them fully.

We may go even further and say that the doctrine of the Atonement cannot be understood apart from its Greek background, which is even fuller and more explicit than the Hebrew. Greek literature contains many references to the surviving primitive conceptions of the removal of sin and of its attendant pollution and consequent evils. Such terms as *katharma, katharsis, katharsion, peripsēma* are full of religious associations. Two late Greek lexiocographers, Photius and Suidas, agree word for word in defining *peripsēma* ("offscouring," in the New Testament): "Thus they addressed the girl who was thrown into the sea, each year, for the removal of oppressing evils: 'Be thou our *peripsēma* (offscouring), or our salvation (*sōtēria*) and redemption (*apolutrōsis* = redemption by payment of a ransom).' And thus they cast [her] into the sea, just as if they were making atonement with a sacrifice to Poseidon." [9] It was the primitive conception that the *miasma* (pollution) of a land could be concentrated in a person (a *pharmakos*) who was then put to death (e.g., by drowning or stoning), and so the corruption, i.e., the famine, epidemic, or other evil, could be removed and brought to an end. Or, if the evil was understood to be due to the wrath of an angry god (usually Apollo, Artemis, Poseidon, or Athene), he or she could be placated by the offering. So likewise the martyr prayed for his people in IV Maccabees 6:29 (a Hellenistic Jewish work): "Make my blood their means of cleansing (*katharsion*, usually used of a sacrifice), and as their ransom (*antipsychon*) take my life." In Herodotus, VII, 133–137, the wrath of the divine hero Talthybius, provoked by the murder of the Persian heralds, can be appeased by the death of two men.[10] It is true such conceptions as these, preserved from a more "primitive" stage of culture in the thought

[9] See G. Stählin, "*Peripsema*," *Theol. Wörterbuch zum Neuen Testament*, ed. Kittel, VI (1955), 84; *The Passion of the King*, pp. 28ff., 8off.
[10] See W. W. How and J. Wells, *Commentary on Herodotus* (new ed., New York: Oxford University Press, 1928), II. 178–181; L. R. Farnell, *Greek Hero Cults and Ideas of Immortality* (New York: Oxford University Press, 1921), pp. 326ff.

and literature of Greece, do not completely explain the Christian doctrine of the Atonement; nevertheless that doctrine cannot be explained without recourse to such ideas, which are primitive (i.e., prehistoric) and biological, social, and religious, *not* juridical. It was the juridical idea which triumphed in the end—in the later Middle Ages and during the Reformation and down to the nineteenth century; but the fundamental concept was always the ancient Hebrew and Greek, not the later Roman or medieval.[11]

Thus, it was a deeply rooted conviction of ancient religion that by dying, the right person could give his life to "remove sin," i.e., either its guilt or its resulting contamination. Why this should be so, or how the principle operated, was not understood. Nowhere does the New Testament explain how or why Christ's death became effectual in the removing of sin, though the fact, which was discovered in the deepest Christian experience, was fully recognized. Ancient readers could probably understand such language far better than we can. For, as we have seen, it was assumed (a) that *a burden of guilt* might settle down like a poisonous cloud upon a sinful family or city, as for example where some unavenged murder had been committed. This terrible *miasma* (defilement or pollution) *could be removed*, in the last resort, only by the death of the proper person—e.g., the king or his son or daughter, or a representative group of citizens or even of slaves. Such a sacrifice was not necessarily viewed as an offering designed to appease the wrath of some angry god, but simply

---

[11] See *How to Read the Bible*, pp. 66–73; also my *Introduction to New Testament Thought* (Nashville: Abingdon-Cokesbury Press, 1950), pp. 254–57.

as the appropriate remedy (*pharmakon, katharma,* or *per-ipsēma*) for meeting the requirements of the situation. Thus Oedipus blinds himself and leaves Thebes as an exile. Thus Apollonius of Tyana singles out a beggar in Ephesus to be the *pharmakos* which will ward off the impending plague. Thus Iphigenia's death will counteract the headwinds that keep her father's fleet from Troy. "Expiation" was not necessarily the placating of an angry deity: it was simply doing *whatever was necessary* in order to remove evil and permit normal functioning again. Thus even the land, i.e., the soil, which was polluted by its inhabitants could be expiated (Deut. 32:43); in fact it must be expiated if it is to produce food for the support of those dwelling on it. For the very land, or the city, or house, was thought of almost as a living thing, capable of contamination, infection, and disease.

Another but similar idea was that of the *devotio,* by which, e.g., Decius the Roman general, reciting the proper formula, identified himself with the forces of the foe, then rode into the thick of the battle and in dying carried down with him to the underworld great numbers of the enemy (Livy, VIII. 9). Thus an individual could be identified with a force, or an evil, or a sin, or a guilt; and by suffering or dying—or by both—he could bear it away and render it harmless (cf. Isa. 53, Lev. 16). The identification of an innocent person with the guilty, especially of an unusually holy or righteous person, was viewed as the most effective means of warding off evil and restoring health or wholeness (*sōtēria,* like *shalōm* in the Old Testament = well-being). So by their death the martyrs expiated the sin of their

people (II Macc. 7:37f.; IV Macc. 6:6, 29, 9:20, 10:8,
17:22; Pal. *Sanhedrin* 11. 30c, 28): "The drops of blood
which fell from those righteous men [in I Kgs. 20:35–37]
made atonement for all Israel." [12]

(b) It was a further assumption in ancient religion generally, and not only among the Semites, that *blood possessed
a supernatural efficacy*, especially in removing defilement
and in restoring the broken unity or fellowship between a
god and his people. Thus blood was also offered to the
gods below, and to the souls of the dead, especially the
souls of those who had been murdered or who had died
violent deaths. (See Aeschylus, *Libation Bearers* 400ff.,
Eumenides 448ff.; Euripides, *Phoenician Women* 996ff.,
Hecuba 523ff.; Plato, *Cratylus* 405; Pausanias, III. 16. 9;
Eustathius on Odyssey XXII. 481, "That cleansing takes
place by blood the histories make clear, how even that of
murderers [is possible], who by washing in it have cleansing at once.") The Jewish religion carried this principle to
its furthest point of development, since the Law held that
"the blood is the life" (i.e., of an animal, Lev. 17:11). The
rule stated in Hebrews 9:22b is also found in the Talmud:
Yoma 5a, Menachoth 5b; cf. Philo, *Special Laws* III. 150
(= ch. 28), "Blood is cleansed by blood." This principle
underlies the whole system of animal sacrifice in the Priestly
Code of ancient Judaism. ("Unbloody" offerings, which
were common in the Greek and Roman world, are also
found, e.g., in Num. 15:17–21; but they were not expiatory.)

[12] Cf. Hans Windisch, *Der Hebräerbrief* (2d ed., 1931), pp. 82–85;
J. Behm in Kittel, *Th. W. B.*, Vol. I (1933), 171–76; R. K. Yerkes, *Sacri-
fice in Greek and Roman Religions and Early Judaism* (New York:
Charles Scribner's Sons, 1952), esp. Ch. 5.

Thus the New Testament doctrine of the Atonement presupposes two traditional ideas, the supernatural power of blood and the expiatory value of martyrdom; yet in both respects the doctrine is developed as an *explanation* of a spiritual reality which existed prior to its interpretation, viz. the experience of the forgiveness of sins and of reconciliation with God through union with Jesus Christ. In Paul's letters the emphasis is upon the spiritual fact; in Hebrews it is upon the sacrifice which explains it. And nowhere has the spiritual interpretation of sacrifice been carried further than by the author of Hebrews. The sacrifice of the Son of God was his own self-sacrifice, effected and made effective by his perfect obedience and submission to the will of God. Perhaps the best preparation for preaching on the Atonement, or for preaching in Holy Week, is a careful study of the Epistle to Hebrews.[13]

It is, I fear, some of the medieval and post-medieval, Reformation and post-Reformation theories of the Atonement, rather than either the Biblical doctrine or the great experienced fact of divine reconciliation, that trouble many modern persons. The preaching of the Gospel in Holy Week is a good opportunity for us to set forth the far older and profounder, more human, more realistic experience of cleansing, of sharing in and benefiting by the divine expiation of sin, the sin-bearing and the removal of sin effected by

[13] The best modern commentary in English is by James Moffatt, in the *International Critical Commentary* (1924); see also the Int. and Exegesis by A. C. Purdy in *The Interpreter's Bible*, Vol. XI (1955), pp. 577ff. To the bibliography on p. 595 add O. Michel, in the Meyer Series (Göttingen, new ed., 1955). In my volume on Hebrews in *Harper's Annotated Bible* I have tried to gather together briefly the major insights of modern scholarship. It is beginning to be realized that the theology of Hebrews is on a par with the Pauline and Johannine, and deserves to be taken fully into account in any portrayal of early Christian thought.

Christ, which the New Testament proclaims. Of course, we must have experienced this ourselves before we can be deeply earnest preachers of the message: sin and forgiveness are part of it—the most prominent part—but back of this lies the deeper experience of sin and cleansing, renewal, fresh strength, and a new beginning. It is more than "wiping the slate clean," or "annulling the charges against us"; it is "the power of a new and endless life," it is "the *new being* in Christ," it is nothing less than the literal fulfilment of the psalmist's prayer,

> Make me a clean heart, O God,
> And renew a right spirit within me (Ps. 51:10).

II

The Passion Narrative was probably the earliest continuous narrative from the life of Jesus to be drawn up for use in the Church. It exists in two main types: (a) the Marcan, which is basic to the whole Synoptic presentation, is found in Mark 14–15; (b) the Johannine, which is independent, is found in chapters 13, 18, and 19 of the Gospel of John. It used to be thought that there was a third narrative, embedded in the special material found in Luke 22–23 and nowhere else; but the growing consensus of scholars appears to be unfavorable to that view. Due largely to the influence of the commentary on St. Luke by the late J. M. Creed (1930), it is now thought that Luke's special passion material has simply been added to the basic Marcan pattern, modifying as well as amplifying it. It has often been held, likewise, that the Johannine narrative is based on Mark's account; but this also is questioned by a growing number of scholars, due largely to the influence of the Reverend P. Gardner-Smith's little book, *St. John and the Synoptic Gospels* (1938). It now appears to be more probable that John made use of old tradition—similar in form to that underlying the Synoptics, tradition which he modified, amplified, reinterpreted, and supplemented—than that he took the Synoptic Gospels and rewrote them. This old tradition used in John's Passion Narrative is quite different from the Synoptic in some respects: the Last Supper takes place before the Passover; Jesus dies while the passover lambs are being slain; there is no trial before a Jewish court (the Sanhedrin) but only a private "examination" in the presence of a coterie of Jesus' enemies gathered in the high priest's house at night; the real trial took place before Pilate; and the condemnation resulted from pressure upon Pilate by the Jewish leaders in Jerusalem, chiefly the temple hierarchy. Not all of these details can be attributed to a mystical or symbolical revamping of the Synoptic tradition; some of them are undoubtedly based upon sound tradition. At the same time, the general or "over-all" representation of the Passion agrees with the Synoptic account, and it is possible to gain a fairly clear picture of what took place. Of course, we no longer try to fit together every detail of the four Gospels, as if the four were derived from some much larger picture which somehow fell apart, like a jigsaw puzzle, and which needed only to be fitted together again to enable us to see every piece in its proper place. That is not the way books are written—and the books are human books, even as the Lord they describe is perfectly human. Instead, we have in the four Gospels the compilation of four narratives which can only be described as "traditional"—i.e., they make use of traditional material, which has been handed down partly in oral form, partly in written: first the oral tradition, then the written sources, finally the written Gospels. The authors of the Gospels were human beings, not angels. They wrote human books, which contained the oracles of a divine revelation and the record of a divine life, an Act of God, the Event of Christ, which was both human and divine. They wrote under the limitations and conditions of human authorship, the Holy Spirit using their efforts and supervising the total process, rather than dictating every word as they went along. (The idea of an infallible record is both impossible to maintain and also entirely unnecessary, from the orthodox viewpoint: textual criticism alone makes it clear that we do not have the precise wording of the autographs—but we have enough, all that is necessary to insure the proclamation and propagation of the Christian Faith.)

As viewed by present-day New Testament scholars, at least by a great many, the underlying, basic narrative of Jesus' last days in Jerusalem can be recovered partly by comparing the Johannine and Synoptic accounts, partly (as by the so-called form critics) by analyzing the Marcan narrative and attempting to recover its basic, pre-Marcan pattern.[14] Since Mark is a Roman gospel, written ca. 68

---

[14] On the pre-Marcan Passion Narrative, see my Cole Lectures on *The Earliest Gospel* (Nashville: Abingdon-Cokesbury Press, 1943), Ch. VIII, "Mark's Passion Narrative," and the references contained in the footnotes. To these now add Martin Dibelius, "Das historische Problem der Leidensgeschichte," *Botschaft und Geschichte*, Vol. I (Tübingen, 1953), pp. 248-257; *From Tradition to Gospel* (New York: Charles Scribner's Sons, 1935), Ch. 7; *The Interpreter's Bible*, Vol. VII (Nashville: Abing-

A.D., this latter narrative is probably the old Passion Narrative which was in circulation (in either oral or possibly in written form) in the church at Rome before the Gospel of Mark was written. It does not matter greatly whether it was in oral or in written form; for traditional religious teaching was as a rule thoroughly stereotyped, and existed in a formulation almost as firmly fixed orally as it became eventually in writing. It was this old pre-Marcan Roman Passion Narrative which was later modified, elaborated, edited, and revised by the Synoptic writers; and it was a somewhat comparable pattern which underlay the Gospel of John.

As reconstructed by several modern scholars, and as presupposed by more than one modern commentary on the Gospels, the outline of this basic, pre-Marcan Passion Narrative was as follows:

> It was now two days before the Passover, and the chief priests and the scribes were seeking how to arrest him by stealth and kill him: for they said, "Not during the feast, lest there be a tumult of the people." Then Judas Iscariot, who was one of the Twelve, went to the chief priests in order to deliver him to them. And when they heard it they were glad, and promised to give him money. And he sought an opportunity to betray him.
>
> On the first day of the Unleavened Bread, at evening, Jesus came with the Twelve. And as they were eating he took bread and blessed, and broke it and gave it to them and said, "Take: this is my body." And he took a cup, and when he had given thanks he gave it to them, and they all drank of it. And he said to them, "This is my blood. Truly I say to you, I shall not drink again of

don Press, 1951), p. 866; Vincent Taylor, *The Gospel according to St. Mark* (New York: St. Martin's Press, 1952), pp. 524–26, 649–64.

the fruit of the vine until that day when I drink it new in the Kingdom of God."

And when they had sung a hymn they went out to the Mount of Olives. And they went to a place which was called Gethsemane; and he said to his disciples, "Sit here while I pray." And he took with him Peter and James and John, and began to be greatly distressed and troubled. And he said to them, "My soul is very sorrowful, even to death; remain here and watch." And going a little farther he fell on the ground and prayed that, if it were possible, the hour might pass from him.

While he was still speaking Judas came, one of the Twelve, and with him a crowd with swords and clubs, from the chief priests and the scribes and the elders. Now the betrayer had given them a sign, saying, "The one I shall kiss is the man; seize him and lead him away safely [or securely]." And when he came he went up to him at once and said, "Master!" And he kissed him. And they laid hands on him and seized him. But one of those who stood by drew his sword and struck the slave of the high priest and cut off his ear.

And Jesus said to them, "Have you come out as against a robber, with swords and clubs to capture me? Day after day I was with you in the temple teaching, and you did not seize me. But let the scriptures be fulfilled." And they all forsook him and fled. And a young man followed him, with nothing but a linen cloth about his body; and they seized him, but he left the linen cloth and ran away naked. And they led Jesus to the high priest.

As soon as it was morning the chief priests held a consultation; and they bound Jesus and led him away and delivered him to Pilate. And the chief priests accused him of many things. And Pilate asked him, "Have you no answer to make? See how many charges they bring against you." But Jesus made no answer, so that Pilate wondered.

Now at the feast he used to release for them any one prisoner whom they asked. And among the rebels in prison, who had committed murder in the insurrection, there was a man called Bar Abbas. And the crowd came up and began to ask Pilate to do as he was wont to do for them. And he answered them, "Do you want me to release for you the 'King of the Jews'?" (For he perceived that it was out of envy that the chief priests had delivered him up.) But the chief priests stirred up the crowd to have him release for them Bar Abbas instead. And Pilate again said to them, "Then what shall I do with the man whom you call 'The King of the Jews'?" And they cried out, "Crucify him!" And Pilate said to them, "Why, what evil has he done?" But they shouted all the more, "Crucify him." So Pilate, wishing to satisfy the crowd, released for them Bar Abbas; and having scourged Jesus, delivered him to be crucified. [The soldiers then took Jesus into the praetorium and mocked him.] And they led him out to crucify him.

They brought him to the place called Golgotha (which means the place of a skull). And they offered him wine mingled with myrrh; but he did not take it. And they crucified him; it was the third hour when they crucified him. And the inscription of the charge against him read, "The King of the Jews." And with him they crucified two robbers, one on his right and one on his left.

And when the sixth hour had come, there was darkness over the whole land until the ninth hour. And at the ninth hour Jesus cried with a loud voice, "Eloi, Eloi, lama sabachthani?" which means, "My God, my God, why hast thou forsaken me?" And some of the bystanders hearing it said, "Behold, he is calling Elijah." And one [of them] ran and filling a sponge full of vinegar put it on a reed and gave it to him to drink, saying, "Wait, let us see whether Elijah will come to take him down." And Jesus uttered a loud cry [or, better, a great shout] and breathed his last. And when the cen-

turion who stood facing him saw that he thus cried out
and breathed his last, he said, "Truly this man was a Son
of God."

This brief narrative, or something very like it, was presumably the earliest form of the Passion Narrative to circu-
late in the oral tradition and to get written down not only
as the basis of Mark's Passion Narrative but as the nucleus
of the whole earliest Gospel, which grew up around the
Passion Narrative. First Mark himself and then the later
evangelists amplified this narrative from various sources:
(a) from other sources of tradition; (b) from the Old
Testament scriptures, whose relevant passages were viewed
not only as appropriate quotations but as formal predictions
of what had taken place; (c) from historical probability,
drawn from a general knowledge of the situation; (d) from
dramatic fitness (especially in Luke) or from mystical
symbolism (especially in John); (e) from theological considerations, which were certainly operative from a very
early date, and not only from the date of John; (f) from
apologetic considerations, especially the motive of shifting
responsibility from the Romans to the Jews—the degree of
anti-Judaism reflected in the Gospels is really disconcerting,
in view of our present-day attempt to heal ancient wounds
and restore a sense of brotherhood which has been lacking
for many centuries. Even the earliest evangelist, Mark, in
editing the old Passion Narrative which lay before him, did
not hesitate to shift responsibility for the death of Jesus to
the Jews, not only to the high priests, scribes, and elders,
the "council" in Jerusalem, but also to the crowd, the
common people, the mass of Jews gathered in Jerusalem for

the Passover celebration. But in spite of this, the crucifixion was obviously a Roman penalty, not a Jewish (which would have been stoning), and the facts are clear: Pilate weakly yielded to the pressure of the high priests after a faint attempt to administer justice and set Jesus free. He cared more for his own security as an increasingly unpopular procurator amid a hostile people than he did for the rights of one more unfortunate Galilean.

This starkly simple narrative already carries the overtones that we find in the later, more fully elaborated accounts. Jesus had come to Jerusalem for the Passover. He had been accompanied by enthusiastic pilgrims who hailed him as the Messiah, the long awaited divine—or at least divinely appointed—King of Israel. He had gone to the temple and driven out those who made it a bazaar of trade rather than a house of prayer. This interference with the established rights and prerogatives of the hierarchy led to their opposition and eventually their attempt to get him entangled with the Roman occupation forces in Jerusalem. This was a very difficult thing to do, as Jesus was not a political figure; his conception of the kingdom of God was non-military, non-political; his own messianic self-conception was that of a humble teacher, leader, who waited for God to act and refused to take matters into his own hands. But the situation seemed desperate to his enemies, and so they seized him by night and devised a plausible charge against him—they accused him of being a "robber" or insurrectionist (*lēistēs*, as Josephus uses the term, and as Mark seems to reflect it in 14:48, 15:7, 27). It was they who invented the charge that he claimed to be "King of the

Jews," a popular term among insurrectionists and insurgents, according to the accounts in Josephus; and it was upon this charge that Jesus was put to death by Pilate. The long silence of our Lord as he refused to deny the charges against him seems far more likely to be historical than to be inspired by the story of the Great Sufferer in Isaiah 53:7, who "opened not his mouth." His certainty that the kingdom of God was near at hand, with which he had begun his ministry (Mark 1:14f.), was still an unshakeable conviction; it meant the intervention of God in human history, God's own establishment of his complete sovereignty over the world. Only, he now faced the terrible prospect that not only were all the righteous to suffer (as in Psalm 22 and Isaiah 53) before the final end should arrive, but that he himself was to die by a Roman penalty, crucifixion; his lifelong faith and confidence in God was thus tested to the utmost. Yet he did not shrink from the prospect, but humbly accepted it as the will of God.

The night before he suffered he had taken bread and broken it and given it to the disciples—as a solemn covenant of fellowship, communion, even of identification, which bound them to him and to one another, like the ancient rite of "blood-brotherhood" in the desert. Now they were sacramentally one, bound together by common food and by sharing the same lifeblood. If one suffered, all suffered. If one died, all must die. Thus united in one common bond of blood-brotherhood, they awaited the course of events. It makes no difference that the disciples "all forsook him and fled." That means only that the bond was broken by their cowardice. What the later Church saw in the Eucharist was present at the beginning: a sacramental union with Christ through his broken body and outpoured blood.

Moreover, since his death was evidently the will of God for him, it must have meaning; and in a sacrificial religion like Judaism, rooted in the Old Testament and in hundreds of years of sacrificial worship, that meaning inevitably got expressed in terms of sacrifice. Only, the later theories of substitution, of propitiation, of an *amende* to cover the slighted honor of God, of a measured amount of suffering intended to offset a measured amount of sin—all these later theories are merely attempts to explain or to illustrate the principle of sacrifice. Basically, let us reiterate, sacrifice meant doing *whatever* was necessary to expiate sin and restore the broken relations between the people and their God. As the Maccabaean martyrs could pray that their deaths might be accepted as an offering to "cover" the sins of the nation, so Christ's death could be viewed as an offering, a ransom, an expiation. Such language is symbolic, of course, but within the symbol there is a meaning profounder than any mathematical formula for explaining the "rationale" of sacrifice. So when men looked back to Jesus' death and interpreted it in terms of their own present experience of forgiveness, reconciliation, and restoration to right relations with God, they were not importing into the tradition something novel and alien: the idea, the profound idea, profounder than clear analytical thinking can fathom, the age-old, fundamental religious idea of sacrifice, was there from the start. According to the oldest gospel tradition, this idea, in some form, was present in the mind of Jesus himself.

Finally, the brief old Roman Passion Narrative that underlies Mark 14–15 ends with a great climax, the confession of the centurion. Of course, he was a pagan, and he used pagan language. That he probably later became a Christian does not alter the fact that his words spoken at the foot of the Cross were pagan words: "Truly this man was a Son of God"—i.e., a divine being who had come to earth, or been born on earth, and who died heroically after living to serve his fellow men. It was essentially an expression of deep admiration, but it could easily become a statement of faith, and did so become in the early Gentile Church, for which "Son of God" was a far more comprehensible term than either "Messiah" or "Son of Man." [15] As the Gentile Church took up other titles, such as "Lord" and "Logos," terms that would have been impossible in Christian Jewish circles in Palestine, so the term "Son of God" became the best-known and commonest divine title applied to Jesus in the early Greek-speaking churches throughout the Mediterranean world.

If we should ever discover this little document, the earliest Passion Narrative—we may call it a document even if it existed only in oral tradition—we should be struck with its completeness as well as compactness, its natural climax, and its Gentile Christian point of view—though it rests upon tradition derived from the Aramaic-speaking church in Palestine. It had no account of the Resurrection,

[15] I have explained this point more fully in my *Introduction to New Testament Thought* (Nashville: Abingdon-Cokesbury Press, 1950), Ch. IX, and in the Introduction to Mark in *The Interpreter's Bible*, Vol. VII (Nashville: Abingdon-Cokesbury Press, 1951); more briefly in the introduction and commentary on Mark in *Harper's Annotated Bible* (New York: Harper & Brothers, 1952).

though each of the Gospels either added such a narrative
or (in Mark's case) implied one. But the Resurrection was
not the end of the life of Jesus: it was the beginning of the
life of the Church. Or if it was the beginning of the second
and final stage in the life of Jesus (see Acts 1:1), it was
still no part of the Passion. *We* cannot stop here, of course;
the story of the Passion is incomplete without the Resurrection—as if one were to describe a battle and leave out
the final victory. And so it was with the later Gospels,
which supplemented the Passion Narrative with their accounts of the Resurrection. In our preaching of Holy
Week, we must bear this constantly in mind; devotion to
the death of Christ, to the Passion, which stops short of his
glorious Resurrection, is not Christian preaching or devotion.

As we study the earliest Gospel, that of St. Mark, we can
see how the author has taken earlier material and joined
it together. The "blocks" of material are still recognizable
—the material is not kneaded or woven together, as in the
Gospel of John, whose homogeneity may be compared
with "the seamless robe." And in the organization of the
Marcan material we can make out an arrangement which
follows an early observance of Holy Week, at least of
Good Friday, Holy Saturday, and Easter, with its three-
hour "watches" or vigils. This is something we should not
have expected to find, nor should we have expected that
critics like Alfred Loisy would be the ones to discover it.[16]

[16] See *Les Evangiles synoptiques* (2 vols., 1907–8), or the commentary
on Mark extracted from this larger work (1912). See also E. Klostermann's
commentary on Mark in Lietzmann's *Handbuch zum Neuen Testament*
(new ed., 1926), pp. 156ff.

It seems to imply that the formal observance of the sacred season goes back even farther than we had assumed. But the liturgical significance of the Gospel of Mark, and of all the Gospels, is steadily being more clearly recognized. The Archbishop of Quebec has shown that Mark's arrangement as a whole fits the cycle of the early Christian-Jewish festivals, beginning in the autumn with Rosh hashanah and providing additional lections for Holy Week and Easter: the evidence is on the inner margin of any Greek New Testament which shows the old chapter divisions, still preserved in the great Vatican Codex, B.[17] Professor George Kilpatrick has shown that Matthew also was a liturgical book, and the late Professor Benjamin W. Bacon demonstrated that the discourses in John were appropriate to the Christian Jewish festivals, Passover, Pentecost, Tabernacles, Hanukkah, and round to Passover once more.[18] The Gospels originated in separate pericopes, like those still found in the Prayer Book. These were grouped, strung together, linked one to one by editorial transitions and brief summaries; and it is not surprising that the final result still bears the marks of this origin, and that the use of the Gospels liturgically is very old, probably as old as the Gospels themselves, which were "church books" from the outset. Not only the Gospels but the Epistles were preserved as liturgical books; they had been addressed to churches, for the most part, and had been written for

[17] Philip Carrington, *The Primitive Christian Calendar*, Vol. I (New York: Cambridge University Press, 1952). See also my book, *The Gospels, their Origin and their Growth* (New York: Harper and Brothers, 1957), esp. Chs. 7–9.
[18] George Kilpatrick, *The Origins of the Gospel according to Matthew* (New York: Oxford University Press, 1946), esp. Chs. 4–5; B. W. Bacon, *The Gospel of the Hellenists* (New York: Henry Holt, 1933), esp. Pt. II.

reading in the public services of worship in the little churches about the Aegean, in Rome, and elsewhere. More than that, the Apocalypse was addressed to the seven churches of Asia, and was meant to be read aloud. Finally, as I have tried to show in a recent book on *How to Read the Bible*,[19] the Old Testament likewise is a liturgical book: it was written to be read aloud; it was so read, in the Jewish synagogues and the Christian churches; it was preserved, handed down, translated, expounded, memorized, copied, and recopied as a liturgical book—and it is a great mistake to view it as some secular anthology of "great literature." It is that, of course; but it is primarily and basically a collection of books used in public worship. And this principle should be dominant and determinative in all our study, exposition, translation and interpretation of it.

When the late Burton Scott Easton and Howard Chandler Robbins wrote their invaluable book, *The Eternal Word in the Modern World* (1937), they expounded the Gospels and Epistles as liturgical units. This was precisely the way the New Testament was viewed in the second century, and it was already beginning to be so viewed in the first; some parts of it were liturgical units from the very start, even before the transition from the oral to the written period. The Gospels were not written as biographies or histories, but as accounts of the traditions about Jesus, for use in the Church, for public reading as the supplement to and completion of the Old Testament (which was the Church's first Bible), and for setting forth the Christian message, the proclamation of salvation in and through Jesus Christ.

Early Christianity was far more liturgical than theo-

[19] Esp. pp. 24–30.

logical. It is often treated as a system of ideas, and bright young theologians wrestle with the logical and even metaphysical problems involved—and so do the older theologians, some of the time. But Christianity has managed to survive impossible theological formulations, provided the hearts of men were turned toward the Lord and were warm with love for the brethren as they knelt in adoration before a common Lord. Not all the problems of theology have to be solved before one can worship! And this is a note both of warning and of encouragement for us today, especially in connection with the ecumenical movement— and also for the private Christian who is distressed over the purely negative character of large areas of current theological discussion, where man's hopeless ignorance of God and his equally hopeless spiritual impotence are stressed as if they were the Gospel. For example, a well-known theologian has said, "The Sermon on the Mount is the greatest indictment of human nature ever drawn up." Is that true? How does it compare with Cicero's *Verrine Orations?* Or with Dante's *Inferno?* Or Macchiavelli's *Prince?* But was it meant as an indictment? Surely the Gospel writers, Matthew and Luke, did not so understand it! They assumed— so did our Lord—that people could "hear these words and do them" (Matt. 7:24, Luke 6:47). Another theologian has said, "Jesus and Paul taught the same theology—Jesus' parables are illustrations of Paul's teaching." But is this true? Or is it an attempt to import a theological system into the Synoptic Gospels, something they may be forced to accept but which certainly was not a part of their original meaning or purpose? Another theologian has said,

"Jesus set forth the pure will of God, in order to force men to throw themselves upon the mercy of God." Is that true? Or did he encourage men to rely upon God's gracious mercy and forgiveness, and then try to do the will of God? Did he preach only judgment, or divine mercy, forgiveness, restoration, healing, and the power of a new and transformed life? Still another theologian has said, "The gospel views history as an increasing avalanche of sin and guilt." Is that true? Of course, there are texts that seem to justify the view, but it is not the whole view. The Gospel is good news of salvation, not merely a threat of coming judgment. Jesus is not just one more "prophet of doom," like some of his forerunners in the Old Testament. The prophets whom he most closely followed, men like Second Isaiah and Jeremiah, were prophets of restoration, salvation, and the hope of better things to come—on beyond the approaching judgment. This seems to be forgotten in much present-day "Biblical" theology, which is fifty per cent "Biblical" thought and fifty per cent post-war pessimism, disillusionment, cynicism, and skepticism, and misses the many-splendored assurance of the fulfilment both of human hopes and of divine promises. Needless to say, this is not the teaching of the Church as a whole, but stems from an exaggerated and one-sided interpretation of the darkly Augustinian strain in medieval and reformation theology, revived in these days by a specially intransigent group of followers who identify this particular type of "orthodoxy" with the Gospel.

In our preaching of Holy Week, let us not forget that the Gospel—and the Gospels—are more liturgical than the-

ological. The observance of Holy Week is a liturgical
observance, not an occasion for a series of lectures on theological topics, which can be presented at any time. The
teaching value of such a genuine liturgical observance is
something far beyond lectures and addresses; we must see
to it that the congregation *experiences* this liturgical event,
and does not merely listen to our sermons or expositions
of a set of theological themes. This is their right—as real a
right as that of any group of Christians at any time in
the Church's long history, from the first century to today.
We can make sure of this by paying attention to the prayers
and devotions of our people, as well as to sermons and in-
structions. If you will let me say it, I will conclude by telling you—out of many years of experience—that if I were
privileged to be a parish priest once more I should lay far
more emphasis upon worship, on the teaching of worship,
on the religious instruction that properly goes with Christian worship, than I ever did during the years of my
parochial ministry. The immense teaching value, the formative value, of the liturgy itself, and the tremendous ad-
vantages by way of impression and memory enjoyed by
teaching which has been related to worship, are often over-
looked but are always available. I should also pay far more
attention to instruction in Christian morals—ethics, moral
theology, if you will, i.e., the Christian way of life in the
midst of a non-Christian world, with specific teaching of
the details of its achievement, and definite facing of problems met by people right where they live here and now.
And I should add that Holy Week is one of the best times
in the year to emphasize this combination of worship and
teaching.

CHAPTER SIX

Preaching in Eastertide

BY J. V. LANGMEAD CASSERLEY

THE FACT OF THE RESURRECTION

THE DILEMMA of the Christian preacher during the twentieth-century Eastertide can be very simply diagnosed and stated: the central theme of Christian proclamation is at the same time to many modern people, including many modern preachers, one of the most puzzling problems of Christian apologetics.

It is difficult indeed to combine the forthright proclamation of the Gospel, which constitutes the strength of the evangelist, with that gift for intellectual diplomacy and verbal plausibility which is the chief virtue of the apologist. Yet we can hardly proclaim the Resurrection in the modern world without raising the apologetic question in the minds of at least a sizeable proportion of the congregation. The dilemma is obvious: if we preach apologetically and envisage the Resurrection primarily as a problem for the modern mind we shall be told, and rightly, that our preaching lacks power; if, on the other hand, we confine ourselves to a strong reaffirmation of the Gospel testimony, we shall

157

be accused of being obscurantist and doctrinaire and of ignoring the characteristic intellectual difficulties and scrupulosities of modern men.

Certainly the Christian preacher must undertake both the evangelical and the apologetic task. He must proclaim the Resurrection in such a manner as to demand and secure personal conviction in the minds of those who hear him, while at the same time laboring to sweep away the obstacles to conviction which may still hold back many of the best and most honest people in any modern congregation from the full and final act of faith and testimony. This does not mean, of course, that these two notes of Gospel affirmation and discriminating apologetic must necessarily be combined in any one sermon. Certainly, however, they must be combined in any one preaching ministry at every Eastertide. One of the things that I should like to plead for here is that we should try to conceive and plan our Eastertide preaching as a coherent whole. In modern Church practice the forty days before Easter are much more frequently and widely conceived and treated as a distinct period of the ecclesiastical year than the forty days after Easter. Yet in the traditional language of the Church the phrase "the great forty days" refers not to Lent, but to the period between Easter and the Ascension. Many people are accustomed to preach courses of Lenten sermons; why not a course of Eastertide sermons which aims at doing justice to the whole Easter message in its depth and splendor? In such a course of sermons we could begin on Easter Day itself with the proclamation of the fact of the Resurrection, consider it from the apologetic point of view on Low

Sunday, and then examine its varied implications for man and human destiny on the three or four Sundays which follow. It is some such arrangement of our Easter preaching to which I shall try to supply a theological and philosophical introduction in what follows.

THE EASTER PROCLAMATION

The Easter proclamation is primarily a proclamation about the status of Jesus, about his relationship to human destiny and human history, his place in the cosmos, his relation to and role in the life of the Godhead. It is in the light of the Resurrection that the Church is led to the conclusion that Jesus is the subject matter neither of history nor of psychology but rather that he demands for himself and annexes to himself a special metaphysical science which is a strange blend of phenomenology, of history and perhaps psychology, on the one hand, and ontology on the other. It is because of the Resurrection, which reveals Jesus as essentially the risen Christ, that the "Jesus of history"— meaning by that phrase not the Jesus who was in history but the Jesus who can be reconstructed by historians—will not suffice either as the chief character in Christian history or as the ground of Christian existence, will meet neither the preacher's demand for a subject matter fit to be called a Gospel nor the theologian's insistence upon a Gospel that is also a coherent rationality.

The Resurrection reveals Jesus the Christ as properly and inevitably the subject matter of a metaphysical enquiry. There is some evidence that what we may call the first-blush, relatively unenquiring Gospel-message of the primitive Church contemplated the possibility that the Resurrection was the moment at which God raised the Man Jesus to the status of the Christ. But if there ever was any such suggestion—and perhaps we are wrong to treat the first language of Gospel-proclamation as though it were a rigorous logical language which carefully deduced and affirmed its own implications and was conscious of and consenting to its ultimate consequences—then we must regard this as a passing phase of unbased and unexplored intuition rather than as the first phase of Christian thinking. Very soon—it all becomes quite clear in St. Paul—the Resurrection is more profoundly interpreted not as the divine exaltation of Jesus to a status which was not previously his, but rather as a divine affirmation of that status which was always and intrinsically his, akin perhaps to the heavenly voices at the Baptism and the Transfiguration but plainer and more emphatic. The Resurrection is not only the theme of Christology, it is also the cause which necessitates our having a Christology.

For a Christology is, from the point of view either of Greek logic or of modern scientific methodology, a strange and paradoxical conception. Normally our " 'ologies" and " 'osophies" deal exclusively in universals or generalizations which describe and interpret a whole range of particular instances. The particular instance as such is handled by the human intellect in terms of its own history rather than in terms of the kind of rationale which properly appropriates to itself a suffix like " 'ology" or " 'osophy." Thus there is no "napoleonology," only the history of Napoleon. There may indeed be a cultus of a historical figure like Shakespeare or Abraham Lincoln, but the devotees of such beings stop far short of demanding that they should be evaluated and complimented with a specific " 'ology" all to themselves. To demand a Christology is a unique intellectual proposal which is the measure of the unique impact of Christ upon human existence wherever and whenever human existence recognizes itself as Christian existence. The cause and ground of this proposal both in the New Testament and in the Church until the end of time is the Resurrection. "God hath made him both Lord and Christ, this Jesus whom you crucified."

We notice at once the singularity and exclusiveness of the affirmation: "God hath made *him* both Lord and Christ . . ."; or again, "There is none other name under heaven given among men whereby we must be saved." With the Gospel we pass beyond religion, with its universal spiritualities, just as surely as we pass beyond ethics with its universal imperatives. The Gospel is no more the affirmation that our being is fundamentally spiritual than it is a merely moralistic profession that we ought to be righteous. The Gospel is the affirmation that he, Christ, and he alone, is the Lord of life and destiny. It has often been remarked that the Gospel is good news, not good advice. We must go further than that. The good news is the confession of a singular, astonishing fact. The Gospel is certainly not ethical exhortation, but it is equally important to note that the Gospel is not what we should normally describe as a spiritual interpretation of life and reality. It is the singular affirmation of the singular fact made manifest in the singular event. Of course, this Gospel affirmation has consequences

for human existence—and the unfolding of those consequences is what we call Christian Ethics; at the same time,
it has implications about the character of ultimate reality,
and the expounding of those implications may be called
Christian metaphysics or philosophy; but the primary theme
of the Easter preaching is the fact itself apart from its
ethical consequences and its metaphysical implications.

Some theologians—and many interpreters of Christianity
who would not perhaps quite claim, or possibly even desire,
a title at once so dignified and forbidding as "theologian"—
have raised and discussed the question whether the heart
of Christian preaching is the setting forth of the Cross or
the proclamation of the Resurrection. It is doubtful, however, whether this is a valid or necessary alternative. If
we turn back to what we know of the earliest Christian
proclamation we shall see at once that the Cross and the
Resurrection are drawn together in a single assertion
precisely because they constitute together a single keryg-
matic reality, their unity indissoluble. "God hath made him
both Lord and Christ, this Jesus whom you crucified." If
we had to sum up the fulness of the primitive Gospel within
the limits of a single proposition, we might perhaps do so as
follows: *The Gospel is the proclamation of the Resurrection of the Crucified Messiah.* The Cross answers the question, "Who is it that is risen?" The Resurrection answers
the question, "Which of the multitude of crucifixions which
men have inflicted on each other since the beginning of
time is significant for all time precisely because it is significant in and from eternity?" We know that there have
been many crucifixions without a resurrection, and some

people have believed in resurrections unaccompanied by any crucifixion. In many pagan mythologies we find dreams of a crucifixion followed by a resurrection, but Jesus is the only actual case of so unique a conjunction reported in and belonging to actual history. For the Resurrection is not declared in the primitive Gospel as though it were some kind of vision with which contemplative, spiritual men found themselves confronted in the lower depths of their quiet meditations. The Resurrection is never presented as the unlikely verdict passed upon life by a profound and brooding spirituality. It is always reported as something made manifest to men on the level of their sensuality. It is always something seen and heard, not on some fourth dimension or mystical plane but seen and heard in the tridimensional or physical continuum inhabited by the most earthbound and sensual men. Again, the Resurrection is always reported as something in history and as belonging to history. "These things were not done in a corner." The Gospel does not say that the Resurrection is a mystic, spiritual "truth-of-faith" which may be perceived only by "spiritual men," perhaps because the Gospel does not even presuppose that real men are "spiritual men" in any exclusive and dominant sense. Christianity is suspicious, and rightly in my view, of the somewhat excessive "spirituality" of the non-historical religions. From the point of view of the Christian Gospel, the Resurrection is a physical event and an historical event. I have said that it demands a metaphysical interpretation, but in good metaphysics the reality which demands and receives the metaphysical interpretation is always and necessarily a physical reality. Metaphysics is always concerned with the meaning of the physical, with tracing the physical to its ultimate roots in being. It is not the business of metaphysical thought to conjure up pseudo-realities out of the vasty deep. Its concern is to interpret rightly what we know physically, rather than merely to imagine or speculate upon that which cannot be physically known.

It is at this point that we are confronted with the problem of the empty tomb, which indeed conditions the whole testimony to the Resurrection as we have it in the Bible, even in those passages in which there is no direct reference to it. The empty tomb is not a mere question for history. Of course, it is possible to affirm the Resurrection without affirming the empty tomb. It is a great mistake, however, to suppose that the Resurrection thus disentangled from the empty tomb story is the same event as the New Testament Resurrection, which includes and presupposes the empty tomb. The empty tomb is not an additional detail which adds nothing to the meaning of the great event; which, so to speak, decorates it like a superfluous piece of ornamentation in non-functional architecture. Those who affirm the Resurrection without the empty tomb necessarily find themselves manoeuvred into the concept of a merely spiritual event. You will find such people calling the Resurrection a "truth-of-faith" rather than a truth of history, and certainly not a truth in nature. Whatever else we may say about such affirmations, this is emphatically not the proclamation of the New Testament. In the New Testament the Resurrection is always a physical and historical event. This is what I mean when I say that the empty tomb is presupposed and lurking in the background even in the case of those Resurrection passages which do not refer to it. The Resurrection is never presented as a merely religious event; never interpreted as a theme which demands profound spiritual vision and insight or the epic soarings of heroic faith. It does not belong to a private world of some special kind of religious intuition and knowledge. "These things," once more, "were not done in a corner." The Resurrection is a deed done on behalf of, presented to, man as man, rather than to man as a spiritual being. The Resurrection finds man where he is, on the level of nature and history, for it is only by first finding man where he is and taking possession of his whole natural-historical being that God the Creator and Redeemer can fulfil the ultimate program of both Creation and Redemption by finally taking him somewhere else.

In saying all this I am pleading for the affirmation of the Resurrection in its integrity, as we find it in the New Testament preaching, and in the witness and sacramental life of the Church ever since. I am asking that we should not tolerate any spiritualized substitute for the fullness of the Gospel of the Resurrection. We must not proclaim it as a kind of myth or parable which illustrates a universal spiritual truth, for that would be to ignore the particularities of existence; we must not proclaim it existentially, as an invitation to, or even a provocation of, an interior act of life-binding decision, for that would be to ignore the historical development of the common human nature and each particular man's inescapable participation therein. We must not proclaim it religiously, as a truth of spiritual faith,

for that would be to ignore nature and the place of the
cosmos in God's plan to redeem his creation. Of course,
we are bound to say that the Resurrection is indeed an
event in the interior existence of each converted Christian
man; but this realm of inward personal existence and decision—which nowadays the existentialist philosophers probe
into and analyze so subtly, and venture to interpret so
daringly—is not and cannot conceivably be the whole of
created reality. Redemption, as the Christian understands
it, means the redemption of the whole creation, of the
whole realm of the creatures; therefore the redeeming
event takes place not merely on the level of existence, but
also on the level of history, the common history of us all,
and nature, not just the common human nature but the
common physical nature in which man finds the ground of
his kinship with all other created beings.

Thus the Resurrection cannot be proclaimed in its integrity and total meaning unless it is proclaimed as in-
corporating, presupposing, requiring and necessitating the
theme of the empty tomb, the theme which answers the
question, "What kind of Resurrection have you in mind,
and what do you really mean, when you proclaim the
Resurrection?"

Perhaps it may be desirable at this point to clarify, rather
than merely to define, some of the terms I have been using.
Where one man recognizes in the Gospel of the Resurrection a demanding challenge to an interior act of personal
faith and self-commitment, that is existence; where two
men find in the Gospel of the Resurrection the ground of

their fellowship and mutual collaboration, that is history; when we recognize in the Gospel of the Resurrection an honest and trustworthy testimony to a visible, physical event which actually occurred, then we are on the level of nature. It is this compatibility with nature, this grounding of existence and history in actuality, which keeps existence and history sane. To proclaim the Gospel of the Resurrection in its integrity is to proclaim it on all three levels at once. When I say or imply that the Resurrection is not only, or even primarily, a matter of faith, or a "faith-truth" rather than a historical truth, it is certainly not my intention to deny that the Gospel of the Resurrection has any connection with deep existential faith and self-commitment. In the New Testament, belief in the Resurrection is not so much a result or fruit of deep faith but rather the cause of it. It is very important that the Christian preacher should not so stress the central importance of faith as to seem to suggest that the main purpose of the proclamation of the Gospel is to evoke faith. Of course, the Gospel demands the response of faith; yet at the same time it would be wholly misleading to say that the main purpose of God in giving us the Gospel, and of the Christ in living out and living through the events which constitute the Gospel, is simply to evoke the response of faith. Oddly enough, it would not be possible to respond to the Gospel with faith if we were to regard the Gospel as no more than a kind of dramatic performance expressly put on for the sole purpose of evoking our faith. The Gospel of the Resurrection can evoke our faith only if it altogether transcends the question of our faith, and is recognized as being radically concerned with the objective purposes of God or, to put the same thing the other way round, with accomplishing the real because divinely ordained destiny of men. It is impossible to make the theme of faith central to the Christian Gospel because faith could never in any circumstances be central. Faith, in the nature of the case, is always a response to a stimulus. In and for the act of faith it is always the objective actuality to which the act of faith is a response which is central. In its own consciousness of itself faith is always adjectival and peripheral.

This seems so obvious when one puts it into words, yet how many Christian thinkers today seem to ignore it! There are so many contemporary Christian writers who vehemently proclaim themselves neo-reformed or children of the great reformers, vehemently, indeed, but in so stilted a prose and complex a vocabulary that I sometimes wonder whether the reformers would recognize them if they saw them, nor can I altogether suppress my own lingering doubts as to their true paternity. For myself, and in this at least I believe that I have something in common with the majority of those who sit in our churches and listen to our sermons, I could put no faith in a "faith-truth." The only kind of truth which can provoke and stimulate and sustain faith is the kind of truth which would be just as true even if I had no faith in it at all. This, at all events, is the way in which the New Testament bears its witness to the Resurrection and the way in which the creeds re-echo the Biblical testimony. The liturgical customs of our own Church compel us to preach our Easter sermons side by side with the Easter readings from Scripture and the confession of the Biblical faith in the words of the Apostles' and Nicene Creeds. It is perhaps not unimportant that the faith which we interpret and expound in the pulpit should be recognizably the faith to which the liturgy testifies, a faith not in *a* resurrection, or in any general principle of resurrection, but in *the* Resurrection presented in what I have called its integrity.

Now it is undeniable that to insist on presenting the Gospel of the Resurrection in its integrity, after the authentic Biblical fashion which we may entitle the way of the Creeds, is for a very large number of people to raise the apologetic issue in its most acute form. It is perhaps easier to convince people that this is what they ought to believe if they are not only to be regarded as Christian in the traditional sense of the word but also to experience the full meaning of the Gospel-message, than to convince them that this is what they honestly can believe. There is thus ample room in our Eastertide preaching for a transition from forthright proclamation to the quieter apologetic mood. Of course, it is true that a great deal of our preaching and teaching at other less festal and dramatic periods of the Christian year may indirectly prepare for the Easter proclamation by constantly tending towards an undermining of the prevalent contemporary prejudice against and suspicion of the miraculous. Nevertheless, the preacher in Eastertide can hardly avoid some sort of confrontation with this prejudice as it affects the specific issue of the Easter Gospel.

THE EASTER APOLOGETIC

In general, we may say that the widespread presumption against all miracles is based upon a hypothesis incompatible not only with the Christian doctrine of the creation but also with the Christian account of human existence. This hypothesis may be described as the belief that the creation, which for the Christian means the whole realm of the dependent creatures, the whole realm dependent as well as each of the creatures, must be regarded as a closed system. When this hypothesis or presupposition is, by means of a rather crude synthesis, incorporated into some system of quasi-Christian thought, it is explicitly added or subtly insinuated that God himself wills to regard and treat it as a closed system. The prejudice is indeed a last lingering relic of eighteenth-century deism. The closed system is regarded as cause of itself and interpretable entirely in terms of itself, with the exception of its origination in time and perhaps of the act which causes it to continue to exist. This always was and still is a thoroughly unsatisfactory and self-contradictory hypothesis, for it is not difficult to see that it is impossible for the creation, any realm of creatures, to constitute a closed system, and hence preposterous to suppose that God should insist on treating it as though it were one when in fact it is manifestly nothing of the kind. In any case, theological deism is obstinately pre-Darwinian. It lives and moves and has its being in a world of Newtonian, or rather immediately post-Newtonian, physics, but it was Darwin rather than Einstein who rendered it utterly incredible by showing that this allegedly closed system is open at least towards the future, and constantly moving in the direction of novelties which, once incorporated into the system, may modify its entire character. With a very different imagery, and on the basis of very different concepts, Biblical eschatology implied rather than expressed a very similar point of view. The created world is essentially the world waiting for a resurrection which, by accomplishing its destiny, will make manifest its true nature. Such a world is essentially a world open to its destiny, a world most profoundly interpreted when we see it in the light of its destiny rather than in the shadow of its present empirical actualities. The creation, resting as it does upon the purpose and the initiative of the Creator, cannot conceivably be defined as subsequently closed to that purpose and that initiative. The prejudice against miracles all along the line is thus inherently deistical, and as incompatible with the most honest and open-minded naturalism as with the Bible and the Creeds.

There is a second form of the prejudice against miracles which is perhaps more frequently encountered in theological circles and yet in some ways, and from the theological standpoint, even more disreputable in its theological origins. This is a prejudice simply against physical or nature miracles which is quite willing to contemplate the possibility of spiritual miracles of grace occurring in the mental and existential sphere. Physical or nature miracles are denied while the divine initiative in the realm of our moral and spiritual experience is strongly upheld. The obvious implications of this modified form of the prejudice against miracles are clearly Manichean, and presumably Cartesian

also. Now it is nature conceived as the subject matter of
physics which constitutes a closed system, while nature or
creation conceived as the subject matter of psychology,
sociology, and history is regarded as constantly open to the
divine initiative. This is the kind of thing that no self-
respecting psychologist, sociologist, or historian can be
expected to put up with. His system may be open, but at
least it is not more open or less closed than the physical
system. Indeed, we have every reason to suppose that this
radical distinction between physical and mental reality is a
grave philosophical error which cannot be sustained in the
light either of modern scientific knowledge or contemporary philosophical analysis. More important for us, when
we mate this gross philosophical error to a theology which
suggests that, whereas the mental and spiritual realm is open
to the divine initiative, the physical realm is closed to it,
so that the one realm is somehow more creaturely than the
other, it cannot stand up in the light of Christian orthodoxy
either, for this is indeed and quite plainly the Manichean
heresy. In the Nicene Creed we assert that God is the
"Creator of heaven and earth, of all things visible and in-
visible," that, in other words, these two constitute one creation, a single and indivisible realm of creatures. There is
no room here for any Cartesian distinction between the
material and the mental, still less for any Manichean interpretation of that distinction which at the same time depreci-
ates the material from the standpoint of ethics and over-
estimates it from the standpoint of metaphysics by exhibit-
ing it as less open to the divine initiative and less responsive
to divine power. I conclude that the prejudice against

miracles is in its uncompromising form deistical, and in its
more prevalent and qualified form Manichean. In neither
case is it compatible with authentic Christian preaching,
with the Gospel proclaimed in Scripture or the Faith expounded in the Catholic Creeds. Perhaps I should add that
we do not really escape from Cartesian and Manichean
dualism merely by reconstructing our vocabulary. A radical distinction between the existential and the objective is
in no better case than an equally radical distinction between
the spiritual and the material, if what we mean to suggest
is that the realm and scope of the divine initiative are
somehow less and more restricted than the range of created
being and becoming.

But in saying all this, we are still really thinking in terms
of our remote preaching and teaching in preparation for
the Easter message, rather than of the Easter message itself.
What we have said is important: A persistent and unflagging preaching and teaching of the Biblical doctrine of
creation is the indispensable background of any proclamation of the Gospel-events. The whole created order lies
in the hand of God, completely under his judgment and
entirely open to his initiative. To accept the Biblical and
Christian cosmology is to be ready for the testimony to
and the actuality of miracles wherever and whenever the
redemptive purpose of the Creator, which is one and continuous with his original purpose in creation, requires the
occurrence of miracle. Nevertheless, experience shows that
in our contemporary climate of opinion even people who
may be persuaded to accept the category of miracle in
theory, as having a kind of general rational validity, will

retreat rapidly when confronted with the Christian testimony to any particular miracle, like the Resurrection, and turn their back upon it with a cry of "Impossible!"

What do people mean when they say that a certain alleged event is impossible? Obviously, they do not mean self-contradictory or inconceivable, like 2 plus 2 equalling 5, or a square circle, for the miraculous episodes to which the Christian tradition testifies are not of this character. Nor can they mean "unimaginable," for even if they themselves cannot imagine such an episode as the Resurrection, it is quite clear that many other people can and do. For myself, I rather think that the proposition X *is impossible*, which looks like a positive assertion, is in fact a disguised negative. Disguised negatives are very familiar in Christian theology. Thus we say *God is omnipotent*, when we really mean "God is not limited by the finite limitations of power with which we are acquainted as finite beings"; or *God is eternal*, when we really mean, not anything which we positively envisage, but rather, "God is not subject to the limitations which hedge about and enclose finite temporal existence." But the disguised negative occurs outside theology, and I suggest that X *is impossible* really means, "I am not acquainted with the ground of X's possibility." At this point the believer in the Resurrection might even join hands with the sceptic and admit that he also is not acquainted with the grounds of X's possibility, although when he says this he will presumably mean that he is not acquainted with the immediate ground of X's possibility, for with its ultimate ground in the creative and redemptive purpose of God, no Christian, of course, can disclaim acquaintance.

There is, I believe, real value in this analysis, for it reduces what looks like a metaphysical axiom to the level of a personal confession. There is a great deal of difference between saying X *is impossible*, i.e., that it cannot conceivably happen or have happened, and merely saying that if X happens or has happened the speaker does not know what particular conjunction of circumstances made it possible.

What the modern mind really needs is not an unproven and unprovable hypothesis which rejects all miracles, but a reassurance of the extreme rarity of miracles. On this point, in my view, the Christian preacher and teacher can conformably with Biblical faith reassure the honest inquirer. Miracles like the Resurrection occur very rarely, perhaps uniquely, and this extreme rarity is the ground of their significance. If we have a great many miracles, then the truth would appear to be merely that we have a great many miracles, no more. It is the extreme rarity of the miracle which makes it possible for the miracle to function as a sign. This, after all, is what really matters to the preacher, particularly in the case of the unique miracle, the Resurrection. It is true to say that what matters about such a miracle is its meaning, that which it signifies, but completely misleading to suppose that we could possibly have the meaning without the miracle. For a significant event to signify anything it must first occur. The unsignalled sign is insignificant. The attempt to base an Easter Gospel on the setting forth of an alleged meaning of the Resurrection story without any testimony to its historical actuality is worse than the trumpet which blows an uncertain sound. Here we have a trumpet that blows no sound at all, and a group of impatient warriors who, having despaired of ever hearing it, keep up their courage by making trumpet-like noises through their own pursed lips. Presently I shall be dealing entirely with the meaning of the Resurrection, but not, I think it important to emphasize here, as one who expounds the symbolism of a myth or a parable, rather as one who endeavors to interpret the meaning of an event, knowing that its actuality is the true ground of his or any conceivable interpretation.

THE RESURRECTION AND HUMAN DESTINY

It is perhaps sad to reflect—but there can be little doubt that this is true—that the most widespread impression of what the Resurrection amounts to in its relation to human life and destiny is a pathetic travesty of the Gospel, yet a travesty which has nevertheless established itself in the minds of the majority of faithful Church people sitting in the pews, and perhaps even among no small minority of faithful preachers occupying the pulpits. According to this prevalent but gross underestimate of the depth and scope of the Gospel message, the Resurrection theme, is bound up and preoccupied with the contrast between life here and now and life after death and beyond the grave, and with asserting that the concept which relates the two is one of survival.

Let us consider this question of survival first. Obviously, the Resurrection is presented in Scripture not as an instance of survival but in terms of revival, so that the new life is as much a creative act and gift of God as the old life which we enjoy already. So far as Western philosophy and religious thought are concerned, the idea of survival has its roots, and the ground of its intellectual respectability, in Plato, particularly in the *Meno*, the *Phaedrus*, and the *Phaedo*. The Platonic arguments do not seem very strong or convincing for most of us nowadays, but during the Patristic and Scholastic periods they appeared to the Church's finest and most gifted minds, for reasons which we can quite understand and respect, to be remarkably coherent and cogent. Thus, the classical theologians, drawn to some concept of revival by their fundamental Biblical loyalties and to some concept of survival as honest rationalists, tended inevitably towards an uneasy combination of the two. Thus, St. Thomas Aquinas holds that God could, if he wished, destroy the human soul, so that it is not intrinsically indestructible, but he hastens to add that God will certainly never do anything of the kind. For myself, I should now advocate dropping the conception of survival altogether, as an entirely superfluous notion which plays no essential role in any Christian scheme of things. Like Laplace we can say, "We have no need of that hypothesis." In addition, we must notice that the modern world's notion of survival is closely connected with spiritualism and kindred superstitious cults. Even if, however, we prefer, for traditionalist reasons, to retain the concept of survival, it remains true that the concept of revival by a purposive and creative act of God is always primary. This is the Biblical concept that really matters. Mortal men do not rise from the dead; they are raised up. Even in the case of the human nature of the Christ, the New Testament on the whole prefers to describe it as "raised up" rather than as "rising."

If we cannot relate the life in the world which we know here and now to the risen life in Christ which is our destiny in terms of survival, still less can we give a true account of it in terms of mere continuity. Death and resurrection is a theme of judgment as well as of hope and promise. We hear so much nowadays of the Gospel as a Gospel of acceptance that we are apt to forget the extent to which it is also a Gospel of rejection. God both accepts and rejects us at the same time. He rejects that in us which is not content to rest upon his acceptance of us. The Christian life as we know it now, indeed, is very largely a long drawn-out process of sanctification in which we learn to reject for ourselves that in ourselves which God has already rejected, so that the Christian life as we know it now is necessarily one in which the notes of discipline and purgation to a very considerable extent predominate. We have every reason to say that God will not raise up that in us which he has rejected, which is identical with that in us which rejects him.

Popular dualism splits man up into a spiritual part, destined for survival or revival, usually survival, and a physical part which has no place in the Resurrection. From this point of view it is man's physicality which is left unraised, and the Resurrection of man affirms the priority and integrity in itself of his spirituality. This popular dualism is the underlying presupposition of all the various forms of the Manichean heresy. The Christian preacher at Easter must spare no pains to make clear to his people not only *that* he rejects it but also *why* he rejects it. The physical nature of man is not characterized by the ambivalence of his spiritual nature. In itself, the flesh is always good. Man's spirituality may pander to, overindulge, and fail to submit his fleshly nature to any shapely rational discipline, but the fault always lies with the spiritual nature. The so-called "sins of the flesh" are all sins of the spirit. Spirituality finds within itself a realm of choice and evil possibility which is unknown to the flesh. Evil spirituality is always possible and not seldom actual. Thus, the judgment of God is always a judgment upon and against evil spirituality. It is a complete misconception of divine judgment, as it is supremely manifested in the Resurrection, to interpret it as a refusal to raise up the flesh. Nor must we say that the Resurrection of the body is impossible. What we must say in all honesty is that we do not know the ground of its possibility. I think we must add that we cannot imagine its occurring, and that the efforts of our artists to do so have been inevitably ludicrous. We might perhaps add that still less can we imagine what life will be like after the Resurrection of the body has occurred.

Resurrection thus involves an ultimate judgment upon, and an ultimate purgation of, our spirituality. To that extent it cannot be interpreted in terms of mere continuity. But there is another reason which makes any insinuation of the category of continuity a radically misleading one. Resurrection in the Bible is always closely related to the theme of transfiguration and glorification. It is a fulfilment of human destiny even more than a restoration of human nature. There have been theologians who have tended to treat redemption as though it were no more than a restoration of the nature which was either completely forfeited or gravely, perhaps mortally, injured by the Fall. (Opinions as to the precise consequences of the Fall differ.) But this is to expound the Bible as though the Bible ended with some kind of triumphant return to the Garden of Eden, whereas in fact it does nothing of the kind. The Garden of Eden in Holy Scripture is the symbol of primordial innocence, not of triumphant sanctification. Man in the Garden is innocent, whereas man in the Kingdom will be pure. The difference is absolute. The Resurrection is always towards the Kingdom and never back to the Garden. Resurrection does not merely restore human nature, it accomplishes human destiny, and the accomplishment of a created destiny is just as much a free gift of God as the first calling into being of the created man. "Beloved, *now* are we the sons of God, and it does not yet appear what we shall be." Because the risen life of man cannot be interpreted in terms of mere continuity, it is always important to lay great stress upon this radical Biblical agnosticism. "It does not yet appear what we shall be." St. Paul quotes Isaiah to similar effect: "Eye has not seen, nor ear heard, neither have entered into the heart of man, the things which God has prepared for them that love him." We know nothing except that the transfigured and glorified life which will be given to us in the risen Christ will be even more radically and drastically Christo-centric than the life in Christ which we know in the Church already. "We know that when he shall appear we shall be like him, for we shall see him as he is."

The life in Christ is something we already know in the Church. The eschatological overtones of the Resurrection are not merely future. There has been a great deal of controversy among theologians during the last quarter of a century about the difference between the so-called "realized" and the more obviously "futuristic" eschatology. To a very large extent it has been an idle dispute. In the New Testament the eschatology is both realized and futuristic at the same time. To some extent we already are what we shall be, and we shall be what we already are in Christ in an utterly triumphant and completely explicit way. If we are to use the category of continuity at all in this context, the continuity is not between all of what we now are on earth and all of that which we shall be in the risen life, but between that in us which is already in Christ and a risen life in which we shall be wholly in Christ.

In St. Paul the life which the Christian lives in the Church is not primarily a life lived on the basis of a reverent, respectful, and contemplative attitude towards the Jesus of history as we learn some of the details of his incarnate life from the Gospels. Certainly knowledge about the career of the Jesus of history can greatly enrich and deepen the Christian life as we know it now, but the Christian life as we know it now is nevertheless primarily a life in which we have moved beyond relationship and actually co-inhere in and with the risen Christ as members of his Body the Church. The Christian life is not lived in *relationship* to Christ, it is lived *in* Christ, so that churchmanship, from the standpoint of the New Testament, is not merely the historical and sociological fact of a group of people standing in a particular tradition and belonging to a particular community—still less is it the psychological or existential fact that a number of different people make identical or analogous acts of faith—rather it is the mystical and metaphysical fact of an actual being, a genuine co-inherence in Christ. The obvious analogy is with the doctrine of the Trinity. We being many are one man, one humanity in Christ; we are incorporated into him and he is incarnate in us. And since it is the risen Christ into whom we are incorporated, and the risen Christ who is incarnate in his Church, the sacred mystery of churchmanship demands to be interpreted in terms of the Resurrection, so that the doctrine of the Church, of the mystery of the Church's being and of the mystical meaning of our churchmanship, is one of the essential themes of Easter preaching. Churchmanship, analyzed at this deepest level, is neither an historical fact nor a sociological institution, neither a psychological state nor an existential condition; churchmanship, at this deepest level of analysis and interpretation, is a subtle blend of metaphysics and mysticism, of a mysticism rational enough to recognize its metaphysical implications, and a metaphysic empirical enough to acknowledge that valid metaphysics is always and necessarily grounded upon mysticism, and verified in terms of ultimate mystical experience.

This reference to the mystical condition which is the ground and meaning of churchmanship reminds us of the extent to which all Christian piety is a Resurrection-piety because it is centered upon and made possible by the presence of the risen Christ. Churchmanship is essentially being "alive unto God through Jesus Christ Our Lord." The characteristic piety which arises within and provides the natural expression of this exalted state or condition of human being may be described in summary fashion by the use of two key words, mysticism and liturgy. The piety of those who live and move and have their being in the risen Christ is always and at the same time (a) mystical and (b) liturgical.

The characteristic Christian mysticism is both like and unlike the many varieties of mystical piety which flourish outside it. Insofar as it is genuinely mystical it resembles, or at least closely parallels, non-Christian mysticism. Insofar as it is radically Christian it is unique. It is essentially a Christ-mysticism. We become one with Christ through the completeness of our participation in the height and length and depth and breadth of his Body the Church. It is then for Christ to deliver us up into that unity with the Father which is his already. It is by being made one with him who is one with the Father that we in our turn are made one with the Father. We may call this a mediated mysticism, and we may even speak of man as *related* to the Father through Christ. The mystical condition of incorporation into Christ, and of our resulting co-inherence in Christ, however, obviously takes us beyond relationship, and the term "relation" should never be used in this context. It is a genuinely mystical condition, for we may define the abolition of relationship as the very essence of mysticism. So long as we are thinking in terms of relationship, our interpretation of such a reality is necessarily a merely external and superficial one. In all this, the relevance of the Resurrection is vital and obvious. To the Jesus of history, the Christ of the Gospels, it is true to say that we can only be related, and where Christian teaching and preaching ignores

the Church—or worse, dismisses the Church as though it
were a mere historical and social institution—it is inevitably
reduced to talking in terms of relationship to the Jesus of
history. The Church considered as a mystical reality, as the
theme and occasion and ground of Christian mysticism, is
only possible on the basis of the doctrine of the risen Christ,
of the wide-open humanity of the risen Christ who is not
merely *one of us* or *one among us* but in a very real sense
all of us. We cannot conceivably be *in* the Jesus of history
as we can know ourselves to be *in* the risen Christ. Of
course, it is for us of faith that the risen Christ of faith, in
whose risen life we are even now alive unto God, *is* the
Jesus of history. Indeed, it is the very essence of that faith,
which makes the Christ of faith the Christ *of faith*, to declare that the Christ of faith is the Jesus of history. Nevertheless, we in the Church cannot but understand what it
was that made St. Paul declare, "Henceforth know I Christ
after the flesh no more." What he really meant, of course,
and this we know not by an exegesis of the passage but by
our sharing in the basic experience, is that we know and
recognize the Jesus of history in the Christ of faith. It is
because as we face the risen Christ we can discern the
wounds of the historic Cross and touch the print of the nails
that we know that he who is alive for evermore is he who
once lived and died among us. Nevertheless, the life in
Christ which we now know in the Church is essentially not
a life lived in relationship to what he was in history, but a
life of incorporation into that which he is in eternity. Of
course, we could not know the eternity without the history,
but we frustrate the whole intent and direction of the his-

tory if we misguidedly attempt to have the history without the eternity.

But if the depths of the characteristic Christian piety are inherently mystical, the outward expression is inevitably liturgical. In the depths of the inner life of the Body of Christ, the members of the Body regularly perform together liturgical patterns of action which repeat and are indeed one with the patterns of redemptive divine action which we can discern in the whole Christ-deed. These patterns of corporate human action which repeat, reflect, participate in, and are one with the pattern of redemptive divine action in Christ constitute the very essence of the Church's visible life. It is through these things that we are rooted and grounded in the risen Christ, and here again the Resurrection is essential to the interpretation of Christian action. The meaning of liturgy is another of the essential Easter themes. Thus the pattern of Death and Resurrection is basic to any understanding of Holy Baptism. At the very beginning of their lives, the Church baptizes its newest and youngest recruits into a death, for this death is the clue to the meaning of life. Similarly in the Eucharist, it is the risen Christ who makes known his presence among us, as to the two disciples at Emmaus, in the breaking of bread. If the Eucharist is the commemoration of a death, that is only because it discerns in and behind this particular death the actuality of a life. In the Eucharist we declare ourselves humble and grateful participators in the life of one who died, "and behold he is alive for evermore." Both the baptismal action and the eucharistic action are meaningless apart from the Resurrection.

Thus, in the interpretation of both the characteristic ways of Christian piety, the Eastertide theme of Resurrection is the dominant and controlling concept. Behind the Christian piety, necessitating and sustaining the Christian piety, controlling and directing the Christian piety, always we find the Resurrection. His risen life is become ours, ultimately the only life we can hope for and already the only life really worthy of desire, however difficult we may find it sometimes to desire it. We are the people who know that there is no life for us except the life we live in him and, conversely, no death for us unless—which God forbid!— we die apart from him.

CHAPTER SEVEN

Preaching in Ascensiontide and Whitsuntide

BY W. NORMAN PITTENGER

BEFORE WE THINK specifically of the affirmations which should be preached during the period in the Church year when Christians relive, liturgically, the Ascension of Christ and the Coming of the Holy Spirit, we must state briefly what has gone before. The significance of the Ascension and the gift of the Holy Spirit to the disciples rests upon the significance which we see in the wholeness of the act of God in Christ, for the Christian faith is *one thing*. It is not a series of discontinuous and discrete beliefs, strung along one after another. It is all one thing; and that one thing is life in Christ, life in which Christ is apprehended in faith to be God's focusing of himself in a Man and in the world of men, for man's wholeness of living as the Son of God.

The Christian faith is a faith in God, a faith in God made manifest in human life in Jesus Christ. It is a commitment of the whole of one's self to all that we know of God thus manifest to us. And the consequence of that faith, as self-

187

giving in responsive trust and love, is *the* faith, as a great affirmation. Let me put the affirmation quite simply: the living God, who is the creative and sovereign ruler of all things, has crowned his continuing self-expression and self-giving to men by making his own, in wonderful fulness, the life of man, in the Man Christ Jesus. Here he has, so to say, concentrated his manifold and various working in and for his children by making himself supremely transparent to them, by acting supremely among them, in One who is a brother-man.

"Our wills are ours, to make them thine," writes Lord Tennyson in *In Memoriam;* in the seamless unity of a life once lived among us, the will of man and the will of God were at one, and so that life, human in every respect save sin, or false self-will (which is a defect in our true humanity, a defect in our will, and so is "sin"), that life was indeed the life of God lived among men, in truly human terms. This is the Incarnation, the Word made flesh—which is to say, the very Self-Expression of Divine Reality permeating and penetrating human life.

But that is not all. For in a world in which men are estranged from God, through their self-will, their arrogant pride in themselves and in their human achievement, the Cross is inevitable. Love must suffer. And on Calvary, the obedient and filial love of the Son, his utter willing of the Father's will, was crowned in a splendid act of self-giving. In that love God reigns; for love, to the point of death, is the secret heart of reality—"the Lamb slain from the foundation of the world." Yet through that mystery of sacrificial love, those who are in Christ, whose lives are at-oned

with his, are made at-one with the Father; and by God's
re-creating, through death, the human life of our Lord, we
are re-created in him, so that we live, even now, in the
heavenly places with him, yet with tasks given us in this
world in which, by his grace, we have been placed to do
his will.

All of that is the necessary prolegomenon to Ascensiontide and Whitsuntide. It is to and for those who are thus in
Christ that the message of the Ascension comes, as it is to
them that the empowering gift of the Holy Spirit is made
available. It is to those who are of the community of faith
that this has meaning, for it is to them, and to them only,
that the significance of the act of Christ has come home,
giving them the faith which overcomes the world and opening their eyes to see that the Lord, risen from the dead, is
still with us and has sent upon us the power of the Holy
Ghost to make us become what by that act we are.

What shall we say, then, of the affirmations which the
Christian evangelist, the preacher of the Gospel of Christ, is
to make to his people as they join with him in the yearly
anamnesis, recalling, of Christ's glorious Ascension and the
Coming of the Holy Ghost?

The first thing that should be said is that we are not to
let ourselves get bogged down in the details of these
"events." Whatever may have been true of other periods
in Christian history, we today are in possession of a new
perspective on Holy Scripture—both the Old and the New
Testament. We are not dealing fairly with our people, nor
are we showing integrity of mind in ourselves, if we dis-
count or forget this in our preaching. All too often we

accept, in our studies, the generally agreed results of Biblical criticism; and then, when we get into our pulpits, talk as if these results did not exist at all. The legendary character of much in the New Testament narrative is apparent to us now, or should be, in the light of Biblical study; the stories of the Ascension and of the Coming of the Holy Spirit on Pentecost are obviously very largely in that category. Hence the notion of physical levitation, in the Ascension, and the notion of visible tongues of fire, at Pentecost, are to be seen as evidence of an inevitable mythopoeic tendency, not as reportage of high historical accuracy.

But, on the other hand, it is equally important to insist that the stories about Jesus which we possess, with their legendary elements, are the *only* stories about Jesus that we do possess. Their value for us is that they give us, with the highly poetical images, the truth of what the primitive Church believed to have happened. It is, in a general way, rather like the miracle-stories in the Gospels. We may not think that they are in fact veridical reports; we can be quite certain that a modern observer would have told differently whatever it was that happened and thus gave rise to the tales. Yet apart from those stories we should not have the full account of the impression which Jesus did historically make upon those who companied with him and told about him. We cannot excise them from the Gospels and content ourselves simply with ethical and spiritual teaching. It was not as an ethical and religious teacher only that Jesus impressed those who best knew him in the days of his flesh; rather, it was as one in whom the *dunamis*, the vitalizing power, of God dwelt and through whom it moved to restore men to wholeness. So it is, then, with the narratives of the Ascension and the first Whitsunday. What these stories say, in their deepest intentionality, is essential to our Christian proclamation, not in the precise form and with the exact detail which have come down to us in the New Testament record, but in the true meaning, the profound significance, that is in and behind that form and that detail.

I have labored this point because I, for one, am convinced that the preacher has an obligation to fulfil here. Dean Inge once remarked that the laity have the right to expect two things of the clergy: "to preach the Gospel and to tell the Truth." Sometimes, I fear, we have failed in this regard, precisely because we have not shared with our people what we ourselves know well enough. Of course, I am not advocating, since I am neither a complete fool nor unaware of the danger to devout souls of a ruthless exposure to Biblical critical results, that we should spend our time on the Ascension Day and on Whitsunday telling our congregations what we do *not* believe about the narratives. That would miss the point altogether. What I am pleading is that we should center our preaching in the things that are in fact central, that essentially matter; that we should recognize symbol as symbol, metaphor as metaphor, poetry as poetry, not taking for what we fondly call "literal fact" that which is rather the "truth embodied in a tale."

But we must turn to the positive side of our consideration. What is it that we are really concerned to affirm as we celebrate the Ascension of our Lord and the subsequent gift of the Holy Spirit?

First, as to the Ascension.

Peter Abelard, and St. Augustine before him, saw that the vital point in the Ascension of Christ is that by his "return" to the heavenlies he has been made universally available, to all men and at all times. The same point, indeed, is made by St. Thomas Aquinas, when in answering the question, "Is the Ascension of Christ the cause of our salvation?" he writes that the exaltation of Christ's human nature to heaven makes it possible for him to "send down gifts" upon all men; and, in replying to an objection, in the same article he tells us that our very union with God is involved in the Ascension of him who is our Head, with whom the members of his Body (the Church) are in fact united (*Summa theologica*, Part III, Q. 57, Art. 6).

The days of Christ in the flesh are ended; and, as St. Paul said, if we know Christ only after the flesh, we do not fully know him. The reason for this is that our Lord's work for men includes, as an essential element in it, that lifting of his human brethren to the same relationship with God that he, in his human nature, possessed. Doubtless it is proper to say that we are made by adoption that which he is by nature; otherwise put, we share in the achievement which God and man together wrought in his human life. But that includes not only salvation from sin but communion with God—a communion which begins, here and now, through Christ, as we ascend in heart and mind with him to the Father. And that Christ-union with God, so to put it, is not confined to those who knew him only in Palestine, nor to those who were granted the vision of him as risen from the dead; it is for all men, everywhere, at all times. Christ is no less available to us now than he was when he walked by the Lake of

Galilee, or when he appeared to Simon Peter after his passion and death. And this is part of the "once-*for-all*" quality of the life and work of our Lord.

Furthermore, God knows, sees, understands humanity and our human experience in and through the incarnate life of Jesus Christ. If it be true that the Incarnation means that in our Lord, as nowhere else and at no other time, God identified himself with men in their human experience, this self-identification, in that degree, is not ended with the death of him in whom it occurred. It continues. It is, as we may put it, taken up into the eternal life of the Divine Reality. In a way, then, this is to say that all men—some in potentiality, others in actuality, depending upon their entrance into realized and intentional union with our Lord—are in solidarity with him; he is, as Frederick Denison Maurice was wont to insist, the Head of the whole race. As Head, not just of the Church which is his Body but of all humankind who are one thing in him, he shares with us, from the "heavenlies," the graces which enable us to become what we indeed already in truth are: sons of God, inheritors of his kingdom, "partakers in the divine nature."

Thus, the Feast of the Ascension signifies not only the coronation of Christ in that it is the real Feast of Christ the King—God accepting and vindicating the crown-rights of his well-beloved Son—but also the feast of the coronation of manhood as such. It is our manhood—no other, no lesser, no greater, but our very own—which is eternally established in solidarity with the Divine Reality. So it is that we reign with him in glory, *now* in earnest, *then* in fulfilment. The Feast of the Ascension is, therefore, the vindication of a sound, Christian, incarnational humanism. The shoddy humanisms which regard man, in his estrangement from God, as the measure of things, are shown up for the imitations and frauds that they are; here is true humanism, in which not manhood in its estrangement but manhood as possessed, used, and crowned by the Eternal Word is indeed the measure of things. The Passiontide hymn speaks of Calvary, saying that there "God is reigning from the Tree"; Ascensiontide tells us that Man, manhood in Christ and we in him, reigns from the heavenly places.

All of this has a practical corollary. We might put it in this fashion: Christ's Spirit, Christ's life, Christ's standard of human nature and of human action, are enthroned in the very heart of Godhead. And that means that his humanly expressed Spirit, his humanly experienced life, his humanly enacted standard, are the very secret of Reality, so far as we men are concerned. *This* is the way of life, not because we men commend it and approve it, but because God confirms it and validates it in the Ascension of his incarnate Son.

So much for the Ascension of our Lord. Let us now turn to the coming of the Holy Ghost at that first Christian Pentecost of which we read in the Acts of the Apostles. And once again, let us make sure that we do not confuse the whole matter by inept insistence on legendary detail. Here, quite as much as with the Ascension, we are not so much to de-mythologize, or to re-mythologize, as to do what I can only call *in*-mythologize—that is, seek to penetrate through the story, with all its legendary elements, to the main point which was in fact the experience of the primitive community and is for us too the central and enduring significance in the narrative. That major affirmation is the genuine empowering of the band of believers by a spirit so compelling yet so personal, so deeply in them yet so much a gift to them, that they found themselves forced to identify the spirit with *the* Spirit promised in the prophecy of Joel —the Spirit who would be poured out on all flesh.

The experience of the little company in the Upper Room, as we read of it in Acts, is the experience of the binding-together of man into a profound unity of worship, of service, of love, of strengthening. Nobody ought to think of this as "the birthday of the Church," for the Church— as the New Testament sees it—is the continuation of the true Israel of God, not founded by Christ in any formal sense but refounded upon him and upon faith in him, and in that "refounded" sense given the promises which God was believed to have made to "Israel after the flesh." Those promises, here fulfilled, make of the Church "Israel after the Spirit"—the Spirit-possessed, Spirit-empowered, Spirit-used community. Of this we shall speak again, since in the preaching of the Whitsun Gospel we must indeed speak of the Church of Christ. Yet we must speak of it always in the light of its historical continuity from "the call of Abraham," as the patterns of Christianized Judaism pictured it.

In the "first fine careless rapture" of the initial Christian experience, portrayed for us in Acts, we need not expect to find theological precision. Indeed we ought not to expect to find it. It is only *after* the event, that theological precision is possible. This does not deliver us, however, from the need to be as careful and precise as we can be on the matter.

Who, then, is the Holy Spirit? In the Nicene Creed, he is defined as "the Lord, the giver of life." It is said also that he "spake by the prophets." This means that the Holy Spirit is not a new arrival in the world with the Ascension of Christ, although some modern theologians talk in this erroneous fashion. The Holy Spirit is the "great Amen" in all creation. He is the Spirit who in the creation "moved on the face of the waters"; he is the Spirit who inspired the prophets to proclaim the Word of the Lord; he is the Spirit who moves through all nature and through all men, to conform their strivings to the pattern of their divinely intended perfection. He is not a new arrival with Christ; but with Christ he newly arrived—by which I mean that his universal presence and operation is, through the coming of Christ, intensified—focussed, if you will—just as the universal presence of the Eternal Word of God, the Word "that lighteneth every man," is focussed and his operation intensified in the person of our Lord himself. That is a very brief statement of what the Church's theology has said about the Holy Spirit; but it has, of course, said more. That "more" is the Church's insistence that the Holy Spirit is not simply "in the world," exhausted by his "economy" in the creation, but that he is also "in the Godhead," co-ordinate with the Father and the Son as the eternal principle, mode, relationship of Godhead in which the Father's love for the Eternal Son is returned in the love of the Holy Spirit—and so God is not a monad-like unity but a rich social unity including all that we, in our small way, know and value of sociality as well as of personality.

It is precisely this rich trinitarian conception of the unity of God which gives the Christian understanding of the divine Reality a depth and profundity which mere theism of the unitarian sort can never possess. Yet we must be equally clear that Christians do not think of God as "a social Trinity," a society of persons, in anything like our human sense, although our human experience—in its personal and social aspects—is our way to understanding about God. What we know in our human life, both quite generally and also specifically as lived with Christ in the Spirit, provides us with the material which we must use—we have no other to use—for whatever we have to say about the mystery of the Godhead and God's ways with us his children.

The first thing that I should wish to insist upon, then, is that we take care that we do not limit the work of the Holy Spirit to simply religious matters. It is part of the Christian picture of things to see that any good deed, creative action, discovery of truth, honorable life, is empowered by the Holy Spirit, even though we may not readily recognize him there. When D. H. Lawrence spoke, in a memorable phrase, about "the wind that bloweth through me," he was really describing (although he did not know it) the way in which the Holy Spirit moves in creation and in man to reveal the things of God—which is to say, the truth, the goodness, the nobility, the love, the righteousness, the beauty, which are God's will and way. St. Ambrose once remarked that "every truth is spoken by the Holy Ghost"; and it is a tragedy that many Christian theologians, and many Christian believers, have not been so generous in their thought as the great bishop of Milan.

If we are prepared to have this wider view, then we can become chartered freemen in this great world. For wherever the good is done, truth is found, beauty is created, we can claim this as "belonging to us Christians," to paraphrase another early Christian writer. And why? Because all this is part of the working of that same Spirit who in the Christian life of communion with God in Christ is known with singular directness and intensity.

Which, of course, brings us to the other point. The Holy Spirit is not simply universal and, as it were, pervasive in his operation; he is also intensive and direct in one particular series of actions—namely, in his indwelling and empowering those who are "in Christ." The Holy Spirit is he who in our response to the love of Christ, the redemption wrought in Christ, the life given by Christ, responds through our response. It is he who prays in us, St. Paul said in Romans; it is also he who does in us, through us, by us, with us, that which God would have done. For he compels us, not by coercion but by the persuasion of his love and the urgency of his demand, to give ourselves back to God as God has given himself to us in our Lord. You might say that as the incarnating and revealing and redeeming action of God, through his Eternal Word, varies in intensity until it reaches its focal point in Jesus Christ, so the responding, enabling, ennobling work of God, through his Holy Spirit, varies in intensity until it reaches its focal point in the Spirit known in our self-surrender to the Lord Jesus. That, indeed, is why the Church is called "the fellowship of the Holy Spirit," for it is in the Church —where men live "in Christ"—that we know precisely such intensity and focus.

I can illustrate this by a story about my own childhood— although I hesitate to use the illustration because I have so frequently used it before. When I was a boy I liked to catch the sun's rays in a library reading-glass. The rays were all about me, illuminating, strengthening, giving life and health to grass, flowers, trees, men and women. But when they were gathered in the reading-glass, they produced another result: they set things on fire—a piece of paper or a cloth. So it is that God's working always brings results, of illumination, of healing, of strengthening; but in the focal instance of Christ, they bring a quite specific and new result: the response which is love of God and man, in the power and by the work of the Holy Spirit there released.

And now we must turn to the Holy Church, the community in which the Spirit is thus so decisively at work. While the Holy Spirit is indeed at work elsewhere and otherwise, it is in the Church of Christ that he is specially at work. There is no Christianity apart from the Holy Church. Here we are at one with the New Testament; in the Scriptures to be a Christian *meant* to belong to the new Israel of God, and the notion that one can be a Christian— in any save the most attenuated sense—apart from membership in the Church, is a comparatively modern and, we have the right to say, entirely fallacious notion. What then is the Church?

It is, first of all, the "fellowship of the Holy Spirit," the place where the Holy Spirit is at work conforming men to the Incarnate Word of God and enabling them to appropriate his "benefits"—what he has done for their whole-making and health-bringing. But precisely because the Lord Jesus is one and because the Spirit, impelling us to respond to that Lord, is one Spirit, the result is that the Church is a community, a society, a co-inherence of one believer with the others in a new and holy life. In other words, the Church is what St. Paul called it, "the Body of Christ."

Now despite the disagreement of some theologians, I am sure that the best way to understand what this phrase means is to take very seriously—indeed, as seriously as St. Paul himself takes it—the analogy of a biological organism. My physical body, for example, is a closely knit, inter-penetrating and inter-related arrangement, in which each part and piece receives its meaning and fulfils its function as part and piece, by being the expressive medium or instrument for some purpose of the self. The Church as the Body of Christ, therefore, is the closely-knit, inter-penetrating, and inter-related vehicle by which Christ our Lord works towards the accomplishment of his purposes in the world. And as the Lord is the "Head of the Body," so the Holy Spirit is the informing and conforming life of the Body. It is he who binds it together in unity of response to, and in unity of expression of, Christ. Thus the Spirit is the Spirit of Christ—the nature of his work, the intention with which he works, and the results which follow from his work, are all defined for us by Christ who is the Head of the Church. It is this which gives us the differentia between the working of the Spirit outside the empirical Church and the working of the Spirit within it. Recognizing this distinction, some theologians have mistakenly assumed that there are, so to say, two "spirits"; but this will not do, since God's work in created response is the same everywhere—he is a God of order, not of confusion. It is always difficult to hold together in a *both-and*, that which so easily could be described as an *either-or*; to maintain both the universality and the uniqueness, both the pervasive and the particular, both the general and the special. But we must do this at every point—and above all, perhaps, with the Spirit.

There is a corollary in regard to our belief about the nature of the Church. Professor Tillich has pointed out the way for us, although what he says could be paralleled, in large degree, by what has been said by other and earlier theologians. You will remember his distinction between the Church as a "latent" reality, in that the potentiality of "church-ness" is found in all those areas where the Spirit is at work, and the Church "in its manifestation" as the Christian community of response to Jesus as the Christ. So it is that we must never seek to denigrate that which is not *of the Church manifest* as if it were also not *of the Holy Spirit* or *of the Christ* who is the Eternal Word of God. It is all of a piece; yet there are distinctions and discriminations; in a phrase which I myself like, there is continuity of process with the emergence of genuine novelty. And that novelty, in Christian regard, is the life of Christ and the community of response in the Holy Spirit which is the Body of Christ.

Traditionally the Church has been said to be characterized by certain "notes": unity, holiness, catholicity, apostolicity. We may look at these and see how they fit into the developing pattern of this discussion. The Church is one: it is one, not because we are now empirically united as we hope, please God, one day to be; it is one because the Holy Spirit works in and through all who profess and call themselves Christians to conform them "in the unity of spirit, in the bond of peace, and in righteousness of life" to the one Lord to whom they respond. The Church is holy: it is holy, not because the members of the Church individually, nor the Church in a collective sense, manifest moral holiness; it is holy because the Holy Spirit works in and through the communion of Christians both to set them apart from the world, as it seeks to organize itself without God, and to give them a mission to the world, bringing the "fruit of the Spirit," wherever released, to men in the world. The Church is catholic: it is catholic, not because it falls into some institutional pattern, not even because its Gospel is "universally known and universally applicable"; it is catholic because it is *whole*, healthy, "kath holou" or, *in terms of the wholeness* of God's way and work in Christ, made catholic by the Spirit who is the Spirit making for and bringing wholeness. The Church is apostolic: it is apostolic, not because it has certain structures which relate it to its formative (and therefore, in one real sense, normative) period, important as this may be; it is apostolic because it is *sent* in the power of the Spirit and rests back upon the Spirit-given response of those who companied with Christ in the days of his flesh.

Every action of the Church, in worship and in work and in witness, is similarly to be seen as of the Spirit. The Gospel is preached by the power of the Holy Spirit; the Eucharist is celebrated through the operation of the Spirit; Christian life is itself life in the Spirit and manifests, if the Spirit have his way, the fruit in "love, joy, peace, long-suffering, gentleness, goodness, faith, meekness, temperance." Therefore the Church is ever to be the fellowship in which the Holy Spirit *may* have his way with men; when it *is* this, it realizes and fulfils its function to be the Body of Christ.

Bishop Lesslie Newbigin has pointed out, in his remarkable book on the Church, *The Household of God*, that while we have recognized the catholic or structural element in the Christian Church and the reformed or evangelical and corrective element, we have not yet sufficiently recognized the pentecostal element. The "holiness sects," with all their strangeness, have something to teach us here. It is not in their shoutings of "Amen," nor yet in their claims to "peculiar gifts of the Holy Spirit," that we may learn from them; rather, it is in their insistence that "the Holy Spirit is the possession of Christians," or, as we should put it, that the Church is the Spirit-filled community in which Christians, its members, are to be possessed by the Spirit. A Church which does not know this, share this, live this, manifest this, is a dead Church, be it ever so orthodox in creed, valid in ministry, righteous in conduct.

"In the meanwhile," in the times between the first coming and the second coming of Christ, we who are Christian are not left comfortless. The Holy Spirit has been given, not for the first time but with singular intensity and directness. The Church has been given, where life in Christ by the Spirit may be found. We live, indeed, in hope; but we live by faith and in love—that is, we live in the Spirit of Christ. The communion which we have one with another in the Body of Christ nourishes us in the faith, strengthens us in the love, and encourages us in strong expectation by the hope of the glory which shall be. Life "in the meanwhile" is therefore a joyous life, as Christian life must always be. It is by the Spirit of Christ, known in the Church of Christ, that we can be assured of him whom we have believed and be persuaded that he is able to keep all that we have committed to him, until That Day—the Day "when he shall come again in his glorious majesty, to judge both the quick and the dead."

CHAPTER EIGHT

Preaching in the Trinity Season

BY THEODORE P. FERRIS

THERE ARE three facts about the Trinity Season that are worth noting at the outset. First, it is the longest season in the Church's year, a maximum of twenty-seven weeks and a minimum of twenty-three—almost one-half of the entire year. Second, in this part of the world it comes in the summer when the preaching energies of the clergy are not at their maximum, and the receptivity of the congregation is not at its most sensitive point. And third, the season focuses our attention on the teaching of Jesus. For the other half of the year our attention is fixed on what we might call the teaching *about* Jesus—how he came, and why; who he was, and how he was made manifest to the world; how he suffered and died; how he rose from the dead and ascended into heaven.

These two views of Jesus are two inseparable parts of a single picture. The first tries to put into communicable form what we think and believe about Jesus; the second, what we know about him, the circumstances and events of his life, the way he lived and the things he said. The first looks at him *from above* as the Mighty Act of God; the second looks at him from the ground, so to speak, and tries to answer the question, "What manner of man is this?"

Either one without the other is incomplete, and indeed misleading, for we cannot think and believe anything about Jesus unless we know something about him, and what we know about him depends for its significance upon what we believe about him.

What we know about Abraham Lincoln as an historic personality and Civil War President, for example, gains greatly in significance when we believe that he is the Great Emancipator, the very personification of the American Spirit of Freedom. And what we believe about him would be little more than an empty shell apart from what we know about him, what he did about secession and slavery.

Likewise, on an infinitely greater scale, what we know about Jesus becomes of supreme importance when we believe that he is the incarnate Love of God, yet what we believe about him is not much more than a pious myth apart from what we know about him. In other words, faith and fact are as inseparable as the two indivisible sides of a coin.

Unfortunately, it is almost impossible to keep these two views of Jesus evenly together. We almost always over-expose one to the neglect of the other. For the most part, Christian history has given the pre-eminent place to the aerial view of Jesus. People on the whole have been more concerned about the nature of Jesus than about the character of Jesus. They have spent more time telling people who Jesus was than they have telling them what he was like.

With the rise of historical criticism, about a hundred years ago, the tide turned violently in the opposite direction, and the Christian doctrine about Christ was often completely overshadowed by the brave efforts of the Biblical scholars to rediscover the historic Jesus. Now the tide is turning once again in the other direction. Missions are now often preached in which Christ is eloquently set forth as the Saving Power of God, whom to confess before men is to be saved from sin, with hardly a word said as to the kind of Person the Saviour is, what he said and did—other than die and rise from the dead—and, above all, what he expects of us once we are snatched from the devil's clutches.

Preaching of this kind usually begins and ends with the Epistles, and the preacher's justification for this is that the Epistles came first. To be sure, they did. They came first chronologically, they were written before the Gospels; no one denies this. But before the Epistles were written Jesus lived, and it is a breath of that life that the writers of the Gospels try their best to pass on to us. "I know whom I have believed," one of them wrote. So might they all have written.

To put it in a nutshell, can we say this? The teaching *of* Jesus without the teaching *about* Jesus is like trying to teach a person to swim by giving him a book of rules, attractively illustrated; while the teaching *about* Jesus without the teaching *of* Jesus is like pulling a drowning man out of the water and leaving him on a raft in mid-ocean with no idea of where he is or what to do next.

In this essay we limit our attention to the teaching *of* Jesus, but it must be remembered that apart from the teaching *about* Jesus the teaching *of* Jesus is meaningless, and that the only reason we think of the two things separately is that we are human beings who cannot see the front and the back door of a house at the same time. We can, however, by the miraculous and god-like power of our memory and imagination, keep both doors *in mind* at the same time, and it behooves us to make every effort to do so, especially when those two doors represent the two indivisible views of our Lord and Saviour, Jesus Christ.

Perhaps it should also be noted that whereas we are always in danger of neglecting one or the other view, our most present danger today is to be so preoccupied with the teaching about Jesus, which we have wonderfully rediscovered, that we neglect the other side of the truth, the teaching of Jesus himself. It is altogether a worthy undertaking, therefore, to stop and think how we as men commissioned to preach the Gospel can make the teaching of Jesus real to our people, so that they can understand it, be drawn to it, and to some small degree at least practice it.

It is not an easy task, and the preacher will do well to recognize the difficulties involved at the very beginning. Most of the difficulties are a result of the fact that the preacher lives in the twentieth century and Jesus lived in the first. As you might expect, times have changed. The world is the same and human nature is basically the same, but the ways of living and thinking are vastly different. A considerable degree of translation is therefore necessary if the teaching of Jesus is to make real sense to a modern American congregation.

Take the kingdom of God, for example. What is there in the contemporary patterns of thought that is at all comparable to it? To what shall the modern preacher liken it? The idea of a kingdom as something to be desired is not one that the ordinary American greets with enthusiasm, and the thought of a real king who does anything more than preside at public ceremonies he automatically dismisses as an antediluvian idea. When you begin to talk about a kingdom that is already here and yet is still to come, he thinks you are indulging in double-talk, and when you go so far as to suggest that when the kingdom comes, the world will go up in smoke, he gives up in despair.

Patience is the first rule for the preacher. The man you are speaking to is not deliberately trying to be difficult; he is just being himself, whereas you are trying to be a first-century Hebrew. His thinking has been strongly affected by the Greek way of looking at things, even though he would be the last to know it and might not appreciate it if you told him so. When he thinks of the good life at all, he is almost surely to think of it in terms of another, ideal world, running parallel to this world of flesh and blood, influencing it, and having Platonic intercourse with it, but never meeting it, never becoming involved with it, and going on and on for ever into eternity. Add to this the fact that the idea of the good life in his mind has a strong cast of western materialism according to which bread and butter are the basis of existence, and you can't greatly blame him for his inability to grasp at once what Jesus meant by the kingdom of God.

It will be a great help to you in trying to explain it to him if you know yourself what Jesus meant. At this point the scholars are more likely to confuse you than help you, simply because they have written so much, and approached the subject from so many, and sometimes conflicting points of view, and have come out with so many different conclusions. The only thing you can do is to make your own investigations, with their help, of course; amateurs though you may be, try to think it through for yourself in terms of your own religious experience, and then pray to God that you will come somewhere near the truth.

In my own case, the thought that lies behind any particular sermon on the kingdom of God goes something like this. The concept of the kingdom of God is the instinctive, Hebraic dramatization of the good life. The Jew never speaks in abstract terms, never thinks in theoretical forms. To him God reveals himself primarily in the course of events, what happens from day to day. His doctrine is almost always in terms of drama, and it is natural that when he thinks of the ultimate reality of the good life, he thinks of something happening, something taking place in the political history of his people, against the broader background of the world itself. This gives concreteness to his religion, saves it from vagueness, brings it down out of the skies into the places where men and women really live.

The preacher may well profit by this remembrance of his Jewish forbears, for all too often he talks about God in terms so abstract, and so unrelated to anything that really matters to anybody, that he might as well not have spoken. When he begins to speak about the kingdom of God and the God who is the King, let him remember that, if he is faithful to the spirit of Jesus, he is not speaking about a God who floats forever above the troubled surfaces of the world, but of a God who comes down like the rain, like a thief in the night, like a king returning from a long absence, like a bridegroom who finds only half the party prepared to meet him.

Granted that we are obliged to translate the idea of the kingdom into some such phrase as "the good life," we must do all we can to fill the phrase with as much of the meaning of the kingdom as we can. When we speak of the good life in terms of the kingdom, we are saying that the good life comes from God. Man does not create it; he receives it. He responds to it. His task is to be ready when it comes. It will come regardless, whether he is ready or not. If he is not ready, he will be left out, and it is not likely that he will have a second chance. To be specific, if the good life is thought of in terms of a world of nations more peaceably related to each other because they are suddenly drawn closer to each other by the techniques of science, if it is the will of God, in other words, that his world be in fact one world, and if that divine will is now being expressed by the events of our time, that world will come. Those nations that are prepared to receive it will live, and those who have resisted everything that might endanger their own private security will perish.

This is even more poignantly true, and easier to bring home to the listener, in the life of the individual. Life is

given to him; he is not asked to create it. Things happen
to him; he is not expected to initiate them. He doesn't have
to storm the gates of heaven; heaven comes down to him.
He doesn't have to try to find God; God is constantly trying to find him. This makes a peculiar kind of religious
temperament—not the extreme passivity of the eastern
mystic who makes no move to do anything about himself
or the world, and certainly not the extreme activity of the
westerner who thinks he can build the kingdom of God on
earth if only he keeps everlastingly at it and gets up early
enough to catch the worm, not that at all. It is rather a kind
of alert passivity, never idle, never withdrawing from the
world of action, but always remembering that God acts
first and that man's part is to make the most intelligent and
unselfish response he can to that action.

Those who have achieved this sort of tranquility are
people wonderfully free from the strain that draws tightly
almost every American face. They have a freedom from
anxiety which in no way relieves them from their responsibilities to their families and their world. They are in a
very real sense citizens of the kingdom. They acknowledge
the right of the King to rule; they do the best they can to
obey his will and respond to his desires. And when they
have done the best they can, they leave the rest in his
hands—a hard lesson for Americans to learn, who want
to do it all themselves, and who think that if they don't do
it no one else will, but a lesson well worth trying to teach
if only a half a dozen catch on to it.

Another particular angle that the kingdom of God gives
to the abstract notion of the good life is that the good life

comes at specific times, in particular crises, in special events. God is always with us, so to speak, but from time to time he makes special visitations, often when we least expect him. We have already suggested this idea, but it is worth thinking about briefly, for its own sake. Things don't just go on and on forever in a monotonous repetition of what has gone before. The good life is not simply trying to match the troubled surface of your life with the untroubled sky above. Something happens which reveals either your readiness or your emptiness, and reveals also the character and nature of God.

When Jesus was born something happened. It wasn't like anything else that has happened, before or since. It can't be harmonized with a million other births, or synchronized with a thousand other similar events. It has its unique individuality and stands alone in the midst of all other human events. The other events are judged by this single event in time, and at the same time they depend upon it for their own significance, shining, so to speak, only by the reflection of its light.

This too, is not easy for Americans to understand. They are hospitable by nature, and they want to take in all the religions of the world, see what is good in each of them, make them all variations on a single theme, and be at home with everybody even though they find it almost impossible to get along with anybody who is different from themselves. It seems to them not very broadminded of God to choose one insignificant place, one point of time, and one particular human life in which to reveal the fulness of his glory and love. It sometimes helps to remind them that apparently God works that way; that ancient Greece was only one small acre of the world when wisdom and art there reached such an intensity of expression that they have been overflowing into the whole world to this day, and that Florence was only one of many cities when beauty burst from it in such luxuriant extravagance that people with an eye for beauty have been drawn to it ever since.

The God of the kingdom is not a God who has favorites to whom he caters, but he is a God who chooses certain ones for certain purposes. If a person cannot see this on the great stage of world affairs, he may see it in his own personal life. In one sense, he is aware of choosing his career; in another sense, he is conscious of the fact that his life work has chosen him. Events and circumstances have encouraged him to move in a certain direction; his natural talents have conspired with events to keep him moving in that direction, and his own deliberate response has brought the whole thing to its consummation. He is also aware, in his more reflective moods, that while men make history, history makes men, and that the major factor in the history of any particular epoch is not so much what men do on their own initiative, as on what God does, and then on what man does in response to it.

The good life as we understand it in the kingdom comes, when it comes, to all and for all. In other words, no one can be good all by himself, and no one can be privately saved. The good life as the kingdom grasps it is social, sometimes disturbingly so. Americans cannot be saved, or even be good, apart from the rest of the world; and Americans cannot be saved apart from other Americans, and Chinese! Society is the soil in which the individual grows, and it doesn't do much good to bathe and educate the individual and leave him in soil that can nourish only weeds.

The good life of the kingdom is here now; it is also coming. Americans of the twentieth century find it easy to take the second because they live so much of their lives in the future; they plan for it, save for it, take out social security for it, and put off almost everything that might make life full and rich in order to be sure of a safe and comfortable life that is coming. It is harder for them to see that the kingdom is already here, not perfectly here, of course, but here in the sense of a foretaste of things to come, and sometimes, at least in my experience, in the sense of a real taste of the thing itself. You see it once in a while in a parish church in which the community of those who love the Lord is both a redeemed and a redeeming community. People are virtually raised from the dead, and the living have something real to live for.

When the kingdom comes, it comes the way love comes. It heals; it understands; it forgives; it suffers, and it also enjoys its loved ones. It stirs them the way love quickens them; it judges them in their own eyes the way love shames them; it releases them from the bands that bind them the way love looses a man and lets him go. But love can be rejected, and often is, not without permanent damage to the rejector. The possibility of failure is real and ever present. Decisions one way or another make a difference. The gate can be shut and not opened again; the gulf can be fixed and not easily bridged. The harvest can come and not be reaped, the call can be heard and not heeded.

This, needless to say, is an uncongenial note in the teaching of Jesus as far as our congregations go. The note of urgency is not often heard, not even in the dissonance of the world's most modern music. There is plenty of time, and it doesn't make any real difference what you do anyway; it will all come out all right in the end. There is just enough of an echo of the Gospel of the Second Chance in that to make it devilishly misleading, and it is sometimes hard to make a man see that the forgiveness of God as it is revealed on the Cross is by no means the same as the indulgence of a father who doesn't really care what his children do. In many American families, almost anything goes. In the kingdom not everything goes, not everything, by any means.

One of the most prickly points in this whole matter of the kingdom in the teaching of Jesus is the apocalyptic note at the end. If the very idea of the kingdom is slightly foreign to the average American, the apocalyptic aspect of it is completely fantastic. It is almost impossible for one preacher to help another when it comes to this, for so much depends upon what he himself believes and through what eyes he sees the whole matter. The subject of the Second Coming is one on which there is much disagreement among preachers. The only possible counsel is: know what you think. Some clergy, when asked what they believe about the Second Coming, are forced to admit that they have never thought much about it. And when you talk about it, don't say more than you honestly mean; and above all, don't be vague about it, trying to satisfy everybody and consequently illuminating nobody.

As far as I personally am concerned, the return of Jesus and the coming of the kingdom within a short time after his death and resurrection was one of the mistakes made by the early Christians, for reasons easily understood. Whether or not Jesus himself made the same mistake, I do not know and dare not say. It would not upset me if he had, for he had a human mind and one of the characteristics of a human mind is not omniscience. On the other hand, it would not surprise me if he did not make the same mistake, for his mind and spirit, human though they were, were so far ahead of the rest of men that to some they seemed small, and the fact that he could overreach the framework of his century is not to be wondered at inasmuch as the centuries belong to him. I am satisfied to say that the apocalyptic element in the teaching of Jesus means to the modern American that the world he lives in will never be perfect, that the life he lives will never be the ideal one, that the Utopia he dreams of will never take the place of the U.S.A., and that the kingdom in its perfection lies on the other side of history, breaking in from time to time with almost unimaginable splendor, leading us on to better things, and promising us fulfilment at the end of the story. It should keep us from getting discouraged when things do not go our way, from being disappointed because we expected too much, or from being indifferent because we expected too little.

I found great solace in the comments of Reinhold Niebuhr in reference to the meeting of the World Council of
Churches in Evanston. He wrote:

> The New Testament eschatology is at once too
> naive for a sophisticated world and too sophisticated
> for the simple-minded modern man, who has become so
> accustomed to trying to make sense out of life by meas-
> uring history in terms of some scheme of rational intel-
> ligibility. . . . While the present seems a very strategic
> era in which to restore a part of the New Testament faith
> which has become discredited and obscured, we need
> only to analyze the needs of our generation to recognize
> that it is not particularly redemptive to approach a dis-
> illusioned generation with a proud "I told you so" and
> a fanciful picture of the end of history, or at least a
> picture which will seem fanciful to our generation.
>
> What would be more to the point is to bear witness
> to our faith in terms of watchfulness and soberness—
> of faith and of love, which will appeal to a world in
> the night of despair as having some gleams of light in it,
> derived from the "Light that shineth in darkness."

About a generation ago Dr. Henry Cadbury of Harvard
warned us of "the perils of modernizing Jesus." The
preacher is always tempted to lift Jesus entirely out of his
context and, in an effort to make him real to the people,
make him something entirely different from the person he
really was. He was not a successful American business man,
or a social reformer, or a political crusader (left or right),
and the attempts to make him one are bound to turn out
disastrously. He was a first-century Jew living in an apocalyptic framework of thought and faith, and to try to make
him anything like a modern American is to make him something that he is not.

On the other hand, there is also the peril of not moderniz-ing him. That is, the preacher who is faithful to the text is often likely to lose Jesus altogether by leaving him in the shades of the first century. The sermon then becomes an academic exercise instead of a spiritual experience, a lecture instead of a proclamation. Somewhere between the two ex-tremes the preacher must take his stand. The facts of the New Testament must not be treated either lightly or ponderously, and the Spirit of the Living Christ must some-how shine through everything that is said about him. In one sense, he is a first-century Jew; and we must not forget it. In another sense, he is the Eternal Contemporary and in some strange way is as much at home in the machine age of the twentieth century as he was in the rural setting of the first. Or perhaps we should say that he was not really at home in either, but that men of all centuries find them-selves strangely at home in him.

Although it is not the purpose of this book to discuss sermon techniques or the organization of sermon material, I know from my own experience that the arrangement and presentation of ideas is as important as getting the ideas in the first place, and often more difficult. I am suggesting, therefore, two sermon outlines which may be helpful in a practical way to those who know what they want to say about the kingdom but do not know exactly how to say it.

THE MINISTRY OF JESUS

"Now after John was arrested, Jesus came into Galilee, preaching the gospel of God, and saying, 'The time is fulfilled, and the kingdom of God is at hand; repent, and believe in the gospel." Mark 1:14,15

So the Ministry of Jesus begins
Maestoso: majestic

It lasted not more than three years, and perhaps not
much more than one.

From any point of view it is one of the most decisive events in human history.

For four Sundays I propose to look at this
phenomenal event, beginning today with the
proclamation.

1. Jesus began his ministry with a proclamation, not an
exhortation.

   A. He was following in the great tradition of Hebrew
religion.

      i. "In the beginning God created the heaven and
the earth."

      ii. "I am the Lord thy God, which have brought
thee out of the land of Egypt, out of the house
of bondage."

      iii. "The eternal God is thy refuge."

      iv. "The Lord is my shepherd; I shall not want."

   B. You find the same positive affirmations in art and
science and politics.

      i. "We hold these truths to be self-evident, that
all men are created equal, that they are endowed
by their Creator with certain unalienable Rights,
that among these are Life, Liberty, and the pur-
suit of Happiness."

      ii. "A thing of beauty is a joy forever:
Its loveliness increases; it will never pass into
nothingness."

      iii. A straight line is the shortest distance between
two points.

      iv. Energy equals mass times the square of the speed
of light.

C. The same is true of religion: it begins with great declarations of truth.

    i. We often try to nag people into being good.

    ii. We do better to follow Jesus.
    Tell them
      a. what God is: God is love
      b. who they are: now are we the sons of God
      c. what life can be: and this is life eternal, that they might know thee the only true God, and Jesus Christ whom thou hast sent

II. Jesus began with a proclamation, and it was a proclamation about the kingdom of God.

    A. It is almost impossible to know exactly what he meant.

      i. He never defined his terms.
        a. Everybody knew, in a way.
        b. Like the "American way of life."

      ii. The popular belief was that the coming of the kingdom meant the end of the world.

      iii. How much did Jesus share that popular belief?
        a. There are many opinions.
        b. We are entitled to our own.
        c. But we can't say dogmatically what he thought.

    B. But when you unwrap the proclamation about the kingdom, you have a proclamation about the rule of God.

      i. "Rule" is a harsh word.
      ii. "Sovereignty" is better.
      iii. "Controlling factor" still better.
      All things are under him; prime ministers, bacteria, circumstances, and events.

    C. The point was: the rule of God was going to assert itself in a new order of life, *very soon!*

      i. In fact, it was just around the corner.

ii. In fact, it was already here, like headlights of car.

iii. Therefore, you'd better live accordingly.

III. This is what Christianity has to tell people today. Christianity has a proclamation to make to you:

A. God rules

    i. It doesn't look so

    a. Russia.

    b. The weather.

    c. It didn't look so then: Rome ruled.

    ii. The sun doesn't cease to shine on a cloudy day: the clouds are part of the picture.

    God doesn't cease to rule when men get in his way: their freedom to block him is part of the picture.

    He doesn't brush them aside; he uses them.

    Russia: to challenge our softness—to train us in patience.

    The thing that has got you down: he is using it.

B. God rules, and he rules now. But he asserts his rule from time to time more specifically; comes out from behind the clouds.

    i. Flowering of Elizabethan England.

    ii. The miracle of Dunkirk.

    iii. The stock market crash in 1929.

C. So that, just around the corner, the kingdom is always coming.

    i. The world of international relationships is coming.

    ii. In a sense, it is already here.

    iii. Whatever we do will not stop it.

    iv. The only difference what we do will make is:

    a. If we repent and respond to it, we will be woven into it.

    b. If we do not, we will be wiped out of it.

Conclusion: The Ministry of Proclamation
  The kingdom of God is coming:
    It never came, really.
    Something greater came.
      He came; God came in him.
      A new order of life around him.

"Thou art the proclamation, and I am the trumpet at whose voice the people came."

PRESENT FACT AND FUTURE HOPE

Introduction: The one thing that Jesus talked about more than anything else was the kingdom of God.

> At times he spoke as though it had already come:
>> "The time is fulfilled, and the kingdom of God is at hand." Or,
>> "The time has come: the kingdom of God has arrived."
>> "The kingdom of God has come upon you." "The kingdom of God is within you." "Blessed are the poor in spirit, for theirs is the kingdom of heaven."
> At other times as though it had not yet come:
>> "Thy kingdom come."
>> You are to watch for it; it will come like a thief.

This apparent contradiction has puzzled people: how can the kingdom be both a present fact and a future hope?

Some have explained away the contradiction. But there is another way by which

this puzzling paradox turns out to be an
illuminating principle.

I. Anybody who has ever had a garden knows how a
thing can be both a present fact and a future hope.

　A. A man makes his garden.

　　i. He plows, plants, and cultivates.

　　ii. It is a present fact.

　　iii. All the powers are there operating.

　B. Yet he always speaks of it in terms of the future.

　　i. He is planning to rearrange it; to increase certain plants that do well; change the color pattern; change the fertilizer.

　　ii. His garden is a future hope.

　C. It is the very paradox that makes a good gardener.

　　i. If he has not future hope, his garden will de-
teriorate.

　　ii. If he has only a future hope, it will be constantly
dug up.

He lives perpetually perched on the point of that
paradox: a garden is at the same time a present fact
and a future hope:

II. See if that does not throw some light on what Jesus
meant about the kingdom

　A. The Jews were looking forward to the time when
God himself would rule them.

　　i. They had been ruled by many others.

　　ii. Most of the time they had been misruled.

　　iii. They were looking for the Age to Come.

　B. Jesus told them that the kingdom of God had come!

　　i. In healing power.

　　ii. In kindness and understanding.

　　iii. In moral regeneration.

"His good news was that the Kingdom of God was a present reality." (Manson)

C. Yet, he went on to say, in another sense, it has not yet come.

    i. There are people who have not yet accepted the rule of God, yielded their pride.

    ii. There are whole areas of life where man still pretends to rule.

    iii. In this sense, the rule of God is still only a future hope.

D. So, Jesus lived on the point of this same paradox.

    i. God rules now! He exulted in that.

    ii. God's rule is yet to come! He longed for that.

III. What Jesus said about the kingdom of God throws a flood of light on many a man's life.

A. Some of you are living on dreams of the future: your life is one everlasting postponement.

    i. What you are doing now is preparation: something to be got through.

    You say: when I get through school; when I get out of the service; when I get married and settle down; when my children grow up; when I make enough money to retire: Then!

    ii. Not then, NOW!

    Life will never be any more real than it is now.

B. But you look at your life as it is now:

    i. Flaws; imperfections; knots; unredeemed areas; unresolved tensions; unrealized ambitions; unexplored areas. Is this all?

    ii. Life is not only a present fact; but future hope; the man you may become; only partly released from the mould.

    iii. That future hope lures you on toward something better; that future hope shakes you out

of your lethargy; gives you courage to try
again; it gives another dimension to your life.

Conclusion: The writer of John's Epistles knew what
this meant. "Beloved, now are we the sons of God, and
it doth not yet appear what we shall be; but we know
that, when he shall appear, we shall be like him; for
we shall see him as he is."

Nine of the Gospels appointed to be read on the Sundays
after Trinity are parables of Jesus. The parables are the
stories that Jesus told to illustrate his sermons. Unfortunately, in many cases we have the stories but not the
sermons, and therefore it is not always easy or even possible to know exactly the point that he was trying to illustrate. The stories themselves are short, pithy, human,
realistic, and people always listen to them even though they
may not always understand them.

The nine selected for the Trinity season include some
of the most popular ones, like the Prodigal Son and the
Good Samaritan, and also some of the less popular ones,
like Dives and Lazarus. They range all the way from
stories about the tender side of God's love, like the Lost
Sheep, to the sterner side of the divine judgment, like the
Wicked Servant. This in itself is a suggestion to the
preacher to sweep the whole of the New Testament sky
with the illuminating light of his interpretive word. Some
men hammer away constantly at the judgment of God,
while others linger sentimentally over the tender mercy of
God toward mankind. Both are failing to grasp anything
like the whole nature of God, who in his love combines
both the tender care of a mother for her child and the stern

judgment of a father for a son whose wickedness he can neither overlook nor excuse.

One way to come nearer to a comprehensive and Christian view of the nature of God is to choose deliberately one of the more difficult parables, like Dives and Lazarus, and use it as the basis for a sermon. In the last analysis, it is unfair for a preacher to tell people about the love of God that will search them out and find them no matter how far they have strayed from the fold, and not warn them about the door that can be shut, the gulf that can be fixed and the failure that can be final. The gulf that Dives dug for himself separated him from his fellow man and ultimately from God. This is hell, and this is a real possibility for every man. One need not draw too finely detailed conclusions from the picture of heaven and hell in this story in order to declare that separation from man and God leads ultimately to the torment of isolation, and that this torment can be final.

This sterner note in the parables of Jesus has not been sounded as vigorously as it might have been in recent years. Consequently, it is now being sounded by some interpreters of the Word almost to the exclusion of every other note in the Gospels. The wise preacher will try to steer a middle course and will speak as appealingly as he can about the boy who was taken back home, and also as realistically as he can about the man who came to the wedding improperly dressed and was therefore asked to leave. Both stories represent something true about life.

Every preacher must answer for himself the question, How can the parables be used most effectively in the con-

temporary interpretation of the Gospel? One thing that
ninety-nine out of a hundred preachers cannot do with any
degree of success is to tell the story in their own words.
The words of Jesus are so much more powerful, more
carefully chosen and more deeply buried in the subcon-
scious that any attempt to paraphrase them is usually
doomed to failure. If it is his intention merely to retell the
story with a few casual comments along the way of interpretation, he would do better simply to read the story
as it stands and let it speak for itself. What he can do is to
take the theme which the story illustrates, develop it in his
own way, using the original story as part of his material.

In my own case, I read the story several times, in as many
different translations as I can find. I try to let the story
speak to me and, while I try to get the principal point of
the story as carefully defined as I can (remembering the
warnings of all the New Testament critics, that the parable
is a story with a single point, not an allegory in which
everything including the 'oil and wine' stand for something) I do not close my ears to the overtones of the story,
to phrases like these in the parable of Dives and Lazarus:
"the rich man also died"—the universality of death, common to rich and poor alike; "there is a great gulf fixed"—
who dug it? is there no chance at all that it can ever be
bridged? "neither will they be persuaded"—the refusal of
the growing individual to listen to those who have gone
before, or to be influenced by any supernatural pressure
from above or beneath.

After I have made my own meditations on the parable,
then I read the best commentators I can find. Sometimes I

have to discard my original thoughts entirely. Sometimes they are enlarged and confirmed by what the commentator has to say. Once in a while I cling to them in spite of the commentator.

The three parables in Luke 15 are a case in point. All three stories are about things that get lost, a coin, a sheep and a boy, and the point is that in each case that which is lost is being sought for. In the case of the boy, nothing much can be done until he himself has a change of heart. He is not like the coin that can do nothing but wait for the woman to find it, or even like the sheep who is helpless until the shepherd leaves the ninety and nine and finds him. The boy is a human being with a margin of freedom, and his father cannot find him until he knows that he is lost and wants to be found.

This theme of the father's love for the child, and the child's response of trust and obedience, is second only to the kingdom in the teaching of Jesus, and it must be admitted perfectly frankly that it is infinitely more congenial to the average American Christian than the teaching about the kingdom. The average level of American family life is certainly not high, but one doesn't have to look very far to see examples of family life that reach very great heights indeed. The absolutely unselfish love of a parent for a child, the love that thinks nothing of itself and that is willing and ready to give everything for the object of its affection, whether it is deserving or undeserving, lovable or unlovable, and is also willing to go through the tortures of the damned to save the wayward and unwilling child from destruction, that love is often to be seen and it comes nearer,

I suppose, to the love that is in the heart of God than any other earthly thing. The child's response to a love like that involves, of course, the possibility of rejection or acceptance. He can take it or leave it, rebel against it or welcome it with open arms. He can let himself be blighted by it or blossom bravely in the shining light of it. In the long run he has the freedom to go his own way, either to heaven or to hell. In one sense, he must work out his own salvation, while in another sense he is being saved at the very moment that he is condemning himself to destruction.

Life in the kingdom of God, said Jesus, is something like family life on a worldwide scale. If you can take the picture of a family, embracing a father and mother and several children, and project it further and further until it finally coincides with the boundaries of the universe, with God as the Father and all human beings as the children, then in that relationship, with that God and those people, life according to Jesus must be lived on family terms. We are used to thinking of God as being like a parent, but perhaps it is worth thinking about it for just a moment in passing because some of these things that we think about so continually we think without much freshness or imagination. God is the parent of the human race. The very essence of his being is love, the creative, imaginative energy which goes out to make and remake and sustain lives that can enjoy him. This, you see, came right out of the inner experience of Jesus who felt the reality of God as the Father, not only of himself but of all other human beings, so acutely that he could not live apart from that relationship, and as he thought of God, he could think of him only as a Father caring for his children, and caring for all of them.

It is hard for us to conceive the fact that God cares as much for the innumerable multitudes of Chinese as he does for us, and for the people at the two poles, if there are any there, as much as he does for people at the equator, and that he cares as much for the Mohammedans as he does for the Christians, as much for the atheists as he does for the devout believers, because they are all his children. That thought is worth dwelling on from time to time.

We are all like the children; we are all sons of God, potentially. We all bear upon us some sign of that relationship; we all have latent capacities to become, in fact, the sons that we potentially are. But of course not all of us do become his sons. In fact, some of us are not on good terms with him at all. Some of us rarely, if ever, think about him, consult his will or try to do it. Some are not on speaking terms with other members of the family. So there are a great many human beings who look for their life outside the family of God; they find their natural satisfactions, at least they think they do, not within the family, where they are on the way to becoming in fact the sons of God that they are potentially, but they find it outside in the tangents of life, in the fleeting interests that they think are so satisfying to their bodies and to their selfish indulgences. Others are growing within the family more and more.

One of the things that Jesus is saying is this: the only way you can live happily in the family of God is to live as a member of the family, to trust God the way a child trusts his father, not to fret about the future, not to worry about the next day's livelihood, but to have an ultimate confidence that things somehow will work together for good if you do your share in cooperation; to try to do what God wants you to do; if you have a decision to make to consult not only your own interests, but to say, How does this work in the whole scheme of things and what would God want me to do with this? And then, of course, it means that you treat the rest of the family in the same way that he treats them, with care and understanding, not because you like them, because you do not, always; or because you agree with them, because you will not, always; or because you approve of them, but simply because they are members of the family and he cares about them.

It is only against this family background that the teaching of Jesus makes any sense at all. Listen to it: Love your neighbor as yourself; love your enemy; go the second mile; turn the other cheek; forgive a person not seven times but seventy times seven; bless them that curse you, pray for them that despitefully use you. Why? Why should you love your neighbor who doesn't care a rap about you? Why should you love your enemy when he would knife you in the back if he had a chance? Why should you turn the other cheek and go against the fundamental, instinctive impulse of your nature? Why should you do any of these things, pray for them that despitefully use you? There is no earthly reason why you should do it, no logical, rational explanation of such behavior. The only reason is that that is the way we do things in the family of God. The only reason is that that is the kind of love that God has for you and he expects that kind of love from you. And if you are ever drawn into active membership in this family by your Elder

Brother, you long to enter into the spirit of the family and to do such things simply because that is the way this family behaves.

Second only to the parables in the Gospels for the Trinity Season are the miracle stories. There are eight of them. The preaching value of the miracle stories varies from place to place and from time to time. In the Bible they are invariably told as a sign and evidence of the supernatural. With the change that has taken place in the climate of our thought, there are increasing numbers of people, especially among those who have been educated, for whom the miracle stories are neither a sign nor an evidence of the supernatural. They are far more likely to be convinced of the presence and power of God by the regular operation of the sun than they are by the story of the sun's standing still in order to give advantage to a particular group of people.

In the world of the Bible the unexpected and unexplained is interpreted as the personal intervention of a personal God as a personal favor. In our world we interpret the unexpected and unexplained as natural occurrences beyond the range of our present understanding.

Miracles happen today just as they did two or three thousand years ago. A dying man gets well contrary to all the expectations and predictions of the experts. At the height of a forest fire the wind shifts and a whole town is saved. A chronic alcoholic suddenly and unaccountably stops drinking. A man on a raft in the middle of the Pacific is rescued after six days of drifting. The point is that our interpretation of these events is different from the interpretation of practically everybody who ever lived before the year 1500. The principle underlying the Biblical interpretation is personal control of everything by a personal God. The principle underlying the modern interpretation is impersonal control of everything by an impersonal law.

We are bold to say that both interpretations are wrong. The first is wrong to the degree to which it does not appreciate the regularity of nature which modern science has observed and tried to formulate in terms of natural law, and the second is wrong to the degree to which it does not appreciate that which is beyond natural law, of which the natural law is an expression. As we grow in our understanding of both the ways of God and the ways of the world, we come more and more to see that the universe is operated by laws made by God, and used by him to bring his purposes to pass.

Different preachers will use the miracle stories in different ways. In my own preaching I never try to rationalize a miracle story. I never try to give a reasonable explanation of the feeding of the five thousand, for example. The reason that it was told by each one of the evangelists, and sometimes told twice, was that they thought that it was an unreasonable event. I do not hesitate, however, to point out how legends invariably cluster around unusual personalities, and how stories which begin with a hard kernel of historic fact can grow as they are told over and over, so that a quite normal and natural event eventually becomes an altogether abnormal and supernatural event. Some of the miracle stories in the Gospels are clear examples of this sort of development, stories like the healing of Peter's wife's mother. We must not forget, however, that the personality of Jesus was, to say the least, an unusual one and that the impression he made on his contemporaries was that of a man who could do wonders. Subtract this element of wonder from the life of Jesus and what remains is pale and thin.

The chief value, to my mind, of the miracle stories in the preaching of today is to remind people of the fact that the universe we live in is completely surrounded by mystery, that we can never be completely sure what is going to happen next, that the laws of nature are nothing more than man's attempt to formulate his observations and that in the long run, the mind and purpose of God is supreme, and that he is not confined or completely restricted by his own regulations. Over and above the laws of life reigns the love of God and that love has the power to take the inadequate supplies of life and multiply them until they are more than adequate to our needs. This procedure our finite minds often neither expect nor understand.

The remaining seven Gospels for the Trinity Season are drawn from the teaching of Jesus, mostly from Matthew's Gospel, and especially from the Sermon on the Mount, with two selections from Luke's version of the Sermon. The implications of this teaching we have already dealt with in the former part of this discussion. Needless to say, to deal with them adequately would fill many volumes.

RECOMMENDED READING

BOOKS RECOMMENDED BY DEAN FOSBROKE IN
CONNECTION WITH PREACHING IN ADVENT

C. H. Dodd, *The Apostolic Preaching*. New York: Harpers, 1936.
C. H. Dodd, *The Parables of the Kingdom*. New York: Scribners, 1936.
Burton Scott Easton and Howard Chandler Robbins, *The Eternal Word in the Modern World*. New York: Scribners, 1937.
John Knox, *Christ the Lord*. New York: Harpers, 1945.
E. Lampert, *The Apocalypse of History*. London: Faber & Faber, 1948.
Paul Tillich, *The New Being*. New York: Scribners, 1955.
A. N. Wilder, *Eschatology and Ethics in the Teaching of Jesus*. New York: Harpers, 1950.

BOOKS RECOMMENDED BY PROFESSOR MOLLEGEN IN
CONNECTION WITH PREACHING IN CHRISTMASTIDE
AND THE EPIPHANY SEASON

D. M. Baillie, *God Was in Christ*. New York: Scribners, 1948.
Dom Gregory Dix, *The Shape of the Liturgy*. London: Dacre Press, 1945.
A. Allan McArthur, *The Evolution of the Christian Year*. Greenwich: Seabury, 1955.
Massey Shepherd, *The Oxford American Prayer Book Commentary*. New York: Oxford, 1950.

BOOKS RECOMMENDED BY CANON WEDEL IN CON-
NECTION WITH PREACHING IN PRE-LENT

C. H. Dodd, *Gospel and Law*. New York: Columbia University Press, 1951.
P. T. Forsyth, *Positive Preaching and the Modern Mind*. Chicago: Allenson, 1949 (3rd edition).
Interpreters' Bible, Vol. I. Nashville: Abingdon Press, 1952.
C. W. F. Smith: *The Jesus of the Parables*. Philadelphia: Westminster Press, 1948.

Alec R. Vidler, *Christ's Strange Work*. London: Longmans, Green, 1944.

BOOKS RECOMMENDED BY PROFESSOR NES IN CONNECTION WITH PREACHING IN LENT

Louis Bouyer, *Liturgical Piety*. Notre Dame: University of Notre Dame Press, 1955.

Yngve Brilioth, *Landmarks in the History of Preaching*. London: SPCK, 1950.

William H. Nes, *The Excellency of the Word*. New York: Morehouse-Gorham, 1956.

Ray C. Petry, *No Uncertain Sound*. Philadelphia: Westminster Press, 1948.

BOOKS RECOMMENDED BY PROFESSOR GRANT IN CONNECTION WITH PREACHING IN HOLY WEEK

B. H. Branscomb, *Moffatt Commentary on the Gospel of St. Mark*. New York: Harpers, 1938.

J. M. Creed, *Commentary on the Gospel of St. Luke*. New York: Macmillan, 1950.

M. Dibelius, *Jesus*. Philadelphia: Westminster, 1949.

M. Goguel, *Life of Jesus*. New York: Macmillan, 1933.

F. C. Grant, *An Introduction to New Testament Thought*. Nashville: Abingdon, 1950.

F. C. Grant, *Christ's Victory and Ours*. New York: Macmillan, 1950.

F. C. Grant, *The Earliest Gospel*. Nashville: Abingdon Press, 1943.

F. C. Grant, *How to Read the Bible*. New York: Morehouse-Gorham, 1956.

F. C. Grant, *The Passion of the King*. New York: Macmillan, 1955.

Harpers Annotated Bible: St. Mark. New York: Harpers, 1952; *St. Matthew*. New York: Harpers, 1955.

Interpreters' Bible, Vol. VII. Nashville: Abingdon, 1951.

Joseph Klausner, *Jesus of Nazareth*. New York: Macmillan, 1925.

BOOKS RECOMMENDED BY PROFESSOR CASSERLEY IN CONNECTION WITH PREACHING IN EASTERTIDE

A. M. Ramsey, *The Glory of God and the Transfiguration of Christ*. New York: Longmans, Green, 1949.

A. M. Ramsey, *The Resurrection of Christ*. Chicago: Allenson, 1950.

G. B. Verity, *Life in Christ*. Greenwich: Seabury, 1955.

B. F. Westcott, *The Gospel of the Resurrection*. New York: Macmillan, 1891.

BOOKS RECOMMENDED BY PROFESSOR PITTENGER IN
CONNECTION WITH PREACHING IN ASCENSIONTIDE
AND WHITSUNTIDE

J. F. Bethune-Baker, *The Faith of the Apostles' Creed*. Greenwich: Seabury, 1955.

F. A. Cockin, *The Spirit and the Church*. London: SCMP, 1939.

F. W. Dillistone, *The Holy Spirit in the Life of Today*. Philadelphia: Westminster, 1947.

J. E. Fison, *The Blessing of the Holy Spirit*. New York: Longmans, Green, 1950.

A. Galloway, *The Cosmic Christ*. New York: Harpers, 1952.

C. E. Raven, *Creator Spirit*. Cambridge: Harvard University Press, 1927.

H. Wheeler Robinson, *Christian Experience of the Holy Spirit*. New York: Harpers, 1928.

Charles Williams, *The Descent of the Dove*. New York: Longmans, Green, 1939.

BOOKS RECOMMENDED BY DR. FERRIS IN CONNECTION
WITH PREACHING IN THE TRINITY SEASON

Edward LaB. Cherbonnier, *Hardness of Heart*. New York: Doubleday, 1955.

Edgar J. Goodspeed, *A Life of Jesus*. New York: Harpers, 1950.

T. W. Manson, *The Teaching of Jesus*. Cambridge: Cambridge University Press, 1935.

Alexander Miller, *The Renewal of Man*. New York: Doubleday, 1955.

Willard L. Sperry, *Jesus Then and Now*. New York: Harpers, 1949.

INDEX OF BIBLICAL PASSAGES

INDEX OF AUTHORS

242

11504CB **174**
04-30-02 30978 MC